THE GRATITUDE *Shift*

AN A-TO-Z GUIDE TO RESET YOUR MINDSET & TRANSFORM YOUR LIFE

Jamie Hess

AND LOU ARONICA

ROCK POINT

Contents

Introduction

There have been many books written about gratitude.

Some approach it through science, grounded in the research of pioneers like Dr. Martin Seligman or Robert Emmons. Others offer spiritual wisdom or practical tools designed to help people cultivate a more positive mindset.

This book carries elements of all of those things—but it also comes from somewhere far more personal.

Before I explain what makes this book different, I want to start with a simple truth: Gratitude did not enter my life as a philosophy. It entered as a turning point.

My name is Jamie Hess. Today I am many things: a wife and mother, an entrepreneur, a television personality, a keynote speaker, a coach, and a podcaster.

I am also an addict.

Long before I stepped into the roles that define my life today, I nearly burned everything down. At the time, I believed addiction was the worst thing that had ever happened to me. What I couldn't yet see was that it would become the greatest catalyst for transformation I would ever experience.

Anyone who has walked through recovery—or loved someone who has—understands that within the chaos there is unexpected clarity. Recovery forced me to slow down, to confront myself honestly, and to rebuild from the inside out. It reshaped how I thought about success, happiness, and ultimately, gratitude.

What emerged from that process was a belief that has guided every chapter of my life since: An attitude of gratitude is the heartbeat of happiness.

Not because gratitude eliminates hardship but because it changes how we experience the life we already have. It turns ordinary moments into meaningful ones. It shifts focus from scarcity to possibility. It teaches us to recognize the gifts hidden inside challenges we never would have chosen.

As I began exploring this idea more deeply, I realized that gratitude was not just an emotion—it was a skill. Something that could be practiced, strengthened, and intentionally woven into daily life.

That realization sparked a journey of study and experimentation. I immersed myself in research from positive psychology, explored spiritual traditions centered on appreciation and presence, and began testing what actually worked in my real life–beyond the familiar advice to "just be grateful." This meant learning to shift my perspective during difficult moments to uncover the lessons within them and weaving positive affirmations into my daily self-talk.

Eventually, that curiosity led me to create *The Gratitudeology™ Podcast*, where I sit down with leaders, artists, athletes, and cultural icons to ask two simple but powerful questions:

When did gratitude become part of your foundation? And what made the "switch flip"?

Again and again, I discovered that the shift rarely happened during easy seasons. It emerged through reinvention, adversity, or moments that forced people to reconsider everything they believed about themselves and their lives. Their stories–intertwined with my own–form the backbone of this book.

Inside these pages, you will find twenty-six chapters arranged from A to Z, each beginning with a quote from one of my podcast guests. Together, they explore gratitude from multiple angles: scientific, practical, emotional, and spiritual. Each chapter ends with a short exercise designed to help you apply the ideas to your own life, because gratitude becomes transformative only when it moves from concept into practice.

One of my motivations for writing this book is a quiet frustration I've carried for years. Too often, gratitude is reduced to simple platitudes: "Just be grateful." "Things could be worse." "Write three things down every day."

These suggestions aren't wrong–but to me, they feel incomplete.

True gratitude is deeper. It is active. It requires awareness, intention, and practice.

When it becomes integrated into your thinking, it changes how you respond to stress, how you connect with others, and how you see your own potential.

That deeper relationship is what I call Gratitudeology™—the study and lived practice of gratitude as a framework for growth, resilience, and meaning.

This book is an invitation.

You can read it front to back or open to whatever chapter meets you where you are today. My hope is that you will find stories that resonate, ideas that challenge you, and exercises that help you build a more grounded and expansive relationship with gratitude.

Because gratitude is not about pretending life is perfect.

Gratitude is about learning to recognize that even in imperfect circumstances, there is always something worth honoring—and something worth building toward.

And once gratitude becomes part of how you think, you don't just change your perspective.

You change your life.

A

Ask: How Can I Be of Service Today?

“I love fostering babies because the way I see it is . . . if this small human experiences our home and experiences love, cellularly, if they have that memory of unconditional love by a stranger . . . well, if we could do that more on this planet, I think we’d all be in better shape.”

—Alysia Reiner, Screen Actors Guild Award-winning actor, and activist

*

We've all been told at some point—usually by an exasperated parent—that "the world doesn't revolve around you." Trust me, six-year-old me was *not* interested in that information! But the truth is, the sooner we can get to that realization, the faster we can find happiness.

Many of us have been told that a gratitude practice should look simple: "Write down three things for which you're grateful." But what if I told you that if that's all you do, you're selling yourself short? Jotting something down in a gratitude journal can be helpful for your mindset—but taking action and being of service has the power to change your life.

So, how does being of service *to others* help us *personally* feel gratitude? The answer is actually something I learned in my twenties while going through the toughest time of my life.

I don't know about you, but the idea of helping others didn't come naturally to me. As someone in early recovery from drugs and alcohol, I was most concerned with just getting through the day, totally fixated on what was required to keep me from veering off course. I was too focused on working on myself to have the bandwidth to help other people. That is, until one day a conversation with my sponsor helped me see things from a different perspective.

I'd been invited to an engagement party for one of my girlfriends, and I was thinking about all the ways this party could mess me up. People were going to be drinking there, and I'd been warned to avoid these situations. A common phrase in early recovery is, "If you hang around a barber shop long enough, you're going to get a haircut," so all I could think about was how much of a challenge and how much of a temptation this party was going to be for me. I shared this with my sponsor, expecting her to give me an easy excuse for skipping the event. Instead, she said, "Have you ever considered that this actually has nothing to do with you and everything to do with celebrating your girlfriend who's getting married?"

I'm fairly certain no one had ever said anything like that to me before, and I was speechless. But she wasn't finished.

"What if you showed up at this party that's being given to celebrate *someone else* and didn't just think about yourself? What if you reached out your hand and asked how you could help honor that *someone else*, how you could make that *someone else* feel more celebrated instead of sitting there and thinking, 'How is this going to be for me?'"

I seriously hadn't considered that. But once I did, I actively helped my friend celebrate, did everything I could to contribute to making her day special—and in the process I felt better, because I was grateful for gifts I didn't realize I had to offer, like the ability to get out of my own head and give of myself in ways that made someone else's situation better.

Being of service links us closely to gratitude because it helps us have true appreciation for what we are able to contribute to the world.

It's a beautiful part of our human condition. Giving of yourself gets you out of your head. Giving of ourselves, unselfishly, feels good. In fact, MRI studies now show that altruism actually sparks some of the same brain receptors and chemicals that are associated with pleasure.

My experience taught me how powerful service can be—and I've seen that same truth reflected in others. Someone who truly embodies the commitment to service is Alysia Reiner. I met Alysia at a SoulCycle class and recognized her instantly because she'd starred on the TV series *Orange is the New Black* and won a Screen Actors Guild Award for the role of the warden, Natalie "Fig" Figueroa. Alysia and I got to know each other, and I learned that she wasn't *just* an actor—she was a gratitude junkie, a service seeker, and a humanitarian.

For example, she opened up to me that she and her husband were emergency foster parents, volunteering to take children into their homes and shower them with love for a few weeks when a foster parent is in need of help. And, as if that wasn't enough giving of herself, during COVID, Alysia decided to train to become a firefighter because she realized there was a need for volunteer first responders on Fire Island, where she lived.

Being of service to others is one of the most effective ways to develop your attitude of gratitude.

It does not have to be overwhelming, and you do not have to foster babies or become a firefighter to achieve it!

Simply creating a list first thing in the morning of small, achievable acts of service can set the tone for your day. Doing this first thing means you will have ideas at the ready and won't have to think of things "in real time" when you're at your busiest.

The point is this: We build self-esteem by doing esteemable acts. Being of service fosters a sense of purpose and accomplishment, reduces feelings of helplessness, and improves mood by releasing endorphins.

Performing selfless acts for others gives us a sense of value, builds up our confidence, and shifts our perspective to enhance gratitude.

When I first got into the rooms of recovery, I was there to save my life. I was expecting advice tied specifically to alcohol or substance use, or perhaps something clinical about my new path forward.

Instead, I was told things like, "Come early to the meeting to set up chairs and you'll feel better." When I looked puzzled, they'd follow up with, "And grab a broom afterwards . . . sweeping up will reconnect you with gratitude."

While I had no idea what they meant in those early days, I'm glad I listened. Those little acts of service changed my life and reconnected me with what mattered. I remembered how blessed I was to be able to show up and complete the tasks. I connected with community, and I felt pride and confidence each time I checked a task off the list.

Being of service can come in many forms. From small moments to large actions, it will bring you to a better life, and it is the best starting point for your gratitude journey.

GRATITUDE PAUSE

Morning Routine: Acts of Service

This is a great morning exercise that you can do each day. On a clean sheet of paper, the notes app on your phone, a journal, or wherever you prefer to jot down your thoughts, make a list of three ways you could be of service to others today. It could be something big, or something small. There's no "right" way to do this—just choose things that feel doable for you.

FOR EXAMPLE:

- Calling a friend you haven't seen in a while and asking how they're doing.
- Pulling your chair over to a colleague's desk and offering to help them with their project.
- Spending some extra phone-free time after school with your kids playing outside.

At the end of the day, write down what you accomplished—even if it's just one thing— and how it made you feel.

- Do you feel more connected to gratitude?
- Do you feel more connected to the person?
- Do you feel happy or proud of yourself?

Create a new list each morning and review it each evening. If nothing on your list happened today, that's okay too. Simply notice how the day went and try again tomorrow.

Become Someone Who Learns to Love the Hard Parts

"Life is lived forward
and learned backwards.
Timing and alignment
is everything to me,
and I believe everything
happens as it's
supposed to."

—Brandon Novak, best-selling
author, recovery advocate, and
former MTV personality

*

I was sitting at my desk on an ordinary Wednesday, moving through a workday that looked exactly like every other one. Emails. Deadlines. A packed calendar. When my phone rang, I picked it up without hesitation—unaware that the voice on the other end was about to change my life forever.

It was my mom.

Before I tell you what she said, you need to know who she is to me.

To me, my mom is Superwoman. She has always been my rock and my soft place to fall. She is my mentor, my best friend, and my role model.

Actually, she's been a role model for hundreds of thousands of women across the country too.

You see, my mother is Joan Lunden, television journalist and trailblazer. I grew up on the set of *Good Morning America,* which she co-hosted for nearly two decades. She found out she was pregnant with me just hours after learning she'd landed the job—at a time when pregnant women on national television were almost unheard of. She showed up anyway. To me, she always seemed invincible.

Which is why what she said next felt impossible to process.

"Jamie . . . I have cancer."

The words reached my ears, but my brain refused to accept them. As the weight of her diagnosis settled in, it felt like the floor disappeared beneath me. In that moment, I knew life would never be the same.

Sensing my shock, my mom gently stepped in again.

"I know how you feel," she said. "I felt the same way at first. But then I started thinking."

I could hear one of her signature rockstar reframes activating in real time.

"Jamie, this is an opportunity. I always wanted to follow in my dad's footsteps, but I didn't choose that path. Now, in a way, I get to."

Her father—my grandfather—was a renowned cancer surgeon who died in a plane crash when she was twelve. She once dreamed of becoming a doctor to honor him but fainted at the sight of blood as a teenager and realized medicine wasn't her calling.

"I can bring cameras into the chemo room," she said. "I can show people this is survivable. I can make it less scary. I can help people."

And that's exactly what she did.

Over the next eighteen months, my mom documented her cancer journey with courage and intention. She didn't deny the pain, but she refused to waste it. Letters poured in from around the world thanking her for making something terrifying feel human and navigable.

This is what it means to learn to love the hard parts.

Not because they are pleasant.

Not because they are fair.

But because they hold the seeds of growth. If we are willing to look for them. And it's important to say this: Hard moments are hard for a reason. We all move through them at our own pace, and that's okay.

My mom didn't come up with that response in the moment. She had been practicing that mindset long before she ever needed it. Long before the diagnosis, she learned to stand in hard moments. As one of the first female journalists on television, she faced relentless criticism—but chose to see it as proof she was growing into her purpose.

Whether it's everyday challenges or life-altering diagnoses, reframing begins with a belief that there is always something to be learned.

When gratitude-led thinking is practiced consistently—not just in crisis—it steadies us when life tests us.

This is one of the core lessons I teach as a coach and practitioner of a gratitude-centered life: The more you train your brain to look for the silver lining, the faster it will instinctively go there.

This isn't to suggest that you need to suppress your challenges. Gratitude isn't about denying hardship. It's about refusing to let hardship become the whole story.

The highs and lows of life are scalable. In everyday moments, we often catastrophize, allowing a difficult client call, a tense conversation, or a looming bill to cast a shadow over an entire day.

I've lived this pattern myself.

One challenging interaction can hijack my morning, replaying while I brush my teeth, stealing attention from my children, lingering long after it deserves my energy.

The good news? That loop can be interrupted.

Once I developed a deeply rooted gratitude practice, I learned how to flip the switch faster.

Instead of letting one stressful moment dominate my day, I can reset—sometimes in minutes, sometimes in an hour—by consciously reframing.

For example:

Challenge: A difficult conversation with a boss or family member.

Reframe: An opportunity to practice courage and confident communication.

This doesn't guarantee the conversation will go the way you hope, but it allows you to show up with intention instead of avoidance.

Challenge: Bills due with little money in the bank.

Reframe: A chance to find new ways to live within your budget and perhaps seek temporary help.

This doesn't make the bill disappear, but it shifts the energy from panic to agency.

Challenge: Exhausting toddler behavior.

Reframe: An opportunity to forge a deeper connection to your child and to help them learn new coping mechanisms.

This doesn't make the moment less overwhelming, but it can help you respond with patience instead of reactivity.

Practice this sort of reframing whenever you can, as this will strengthen the muscle for the moments that truly test you.

Among the many powerful stories shared on my podcast, Brandon Novak's stands out as a striking example of learning to love the hard parts. Long before he became an MTV personality, recovery advocate, or best-selling author, Brandon was a skateboarding prodigy. Growing up in a chaotic home shaped by addiction, skateboarding became both his escape and his identity. By just fourteen years old, he was sponsored by Powell-Peralta—one of the biggest brands in skateboarding—and even secured sponsorship from Gatorade, putting him on a meteoric path toward stardom. He was talented, driven, and positioned for an extraordinary future. But when drugs entered the picture, everything changed. By seventeen, Brandon was a full-blown heroin addict, ultimately losing the sponsorships, career, and passion that once defined him.

His friendship with fellow skateboarder Bam Margera would eventually reconnect him to fame through MTV's *Jackass* and *Viva La Bam*, where Brandon's larger-than-life personality and chaotic behavior became part of pop culture itself. But behind the cameras, addiction still had a relentless grip. Brandon's life spiraled through homelessness, repeated treatment stays, overdoses, and devastating losses. Time and time again, he found himself at rock bottom.

Yet it was within those darkest moments that Brandon began to uncover something powerful: His pain could either destroy him, or it could teach him.

Slowly, he chose the latter.

"It hit me like a ton of bricks that I am the common denominator in every one of my problems," he explained to me in our interview. "And maybe if I just get out of my way, I might stand a chance, right?" he continued. "I started to become accountable for my actions."

In that moment he took ownership and began to learn from his challenges, he found a new path forward. Today, Brandon has transformed his deepest struggles into his greatest service as a motivational speaker, Certified Interventionist, and owner of Redemption Addiction Treatment Center and Novak's House Sober Living. The same hard parts that once nearly took his life became the foundation of his purpose—helping others find recovery, hope, and healing.

His story is a profound reminder that our greatest pain can become our greatest preparation.

Loving the hard parts doesn't mean wishing for suffering; it means recognizing that within life's most difficult chapters often lies the wisdom, resilience, and clarity that shape who we are meant to become. Brandon Novak's life is proof that even the most broken paths can ultimately lead to extraordinary purpose.

GRATITUDE REFLECTION

Whether it's everyday challenges or life-altering diagnoses, reframing begins with a belief that there is always something to be learned.

GRATITUDE PAUSE

The Inner Reframe

When we are faced with big challenges, we are often too caught up in the moment to find the tools we need to address them. The key, then, is to practice on the small stuff—the daily annoyances, the occasional irritations—so you build the habit of finding growth *inside* a challenge. Try this reframing exercise.

STEP 1: NAME THE HARD THING.

What's currently frustrating you or making your daily life more difficult than it needs to be?

Right now, I'm struggling with ________.

STEP 2: ACKNOWLEDGE THE FEELING—WITHOUT FIXING IT.

This isn't about bypassing emotion. Name it honestly.

This situation makes me feel ________.

STEP 3: ASK THE REFRAME QUESTION.

Without forcing positivity, ask gently: If this experience were cracking me open from the inside, what might it be teaching me?

Possible answers might include:

Patience

Boundaries

Courage

Self-trust

Better communication

A new direction

STEP 4: COMPLETE THIS SENTENCE:

One way this challenge could be shaping me for what's next is

________.

Over time, this small daily practice helps you meet life's challenges with more steadiness and self-trust.

GRATITUDE REMINDER

I don't need to like this moment—I only need to learn from it.

C

Connect With Those Around You

“We were never designed to carry it all on our own. The very thing we hesitate to reach for—connection—is often the bridge that helps us rise, heal, and keep going.”

—Jessica Janzen,
motivational speaker, author,
and philanthropist

*

Gratitude is often thought of as a solitary practice. While starting a gratitude journal can be a powerful place to begin, it's only a part of the picture. What if I told you that making gratitude a shared experience isn't just helpful—it's essential?

Here's the unfortunate truth: Our brains are not naturally wired for gratitude. They were designed to keep us alive—to scan the environment for threats, danger, and what could go wrong. Thousands of years ago, that meant watching out for predators like saber-toothed tigers. Today, it shows up as an endless mental loop of worries, frustrations, and worst-case scenarios.

Our default setting is to notice what's wrong, not what's right.

That's why advice like "just be grateful" can feel frustrating and even dismissive. You may genuinely want to focus on gratitude, but when your neural pathways are trained to deliver bad news all day long, staying in a grateful mindset can feel exhausting.

This is where community becomes the secret weapon.

When we invite other people into our gratitude practice, everything changes.

Community creates accountability, the same way a workout buddy gets you to the gym on days you'd rather stay on the couch.

You might know that gratitude is good for you, but life gets busy. Days slip by. Intentions fade.

But when other people are involved—when there's a group text, a shared ritual, or a standing moment of connection—gratitude becomes something you *show up for*. You've created structure. Expectation. Commitment.

And you're far less likely to punk out.

Community also amplifies experience. When we celebrate something together, our appreciation deepens.

Seeing gratitude reflected back to you through someone else's eyes reinforces its power. You don't just feel grateful—you witness gratitude at work in real time.

For me, staying connected through a long-running gratitude group chat has offered both beautiful moments and sobering wake-up calls. The group includes people I met in early recovery, and we've remained connected over the years. Some have gone on to live big, beautiful lives. Others have struggled. The spectrum of experiences has been wide and humbling.

One day not long ago, I was having what I considered a terrible day. My kids were talking back. I was behind on a few bills. A client was unhappy and made sure I felt it. Everything felt heavy and unfair.

Then I checked my mailbox.

As I shuffled through the envelopes, one stopped me cold.

Federal Prison Camp

Inmate Number 974324

It was a letter from one of my gratitude-group buddies. His name is Derek.

Derek had relapsed and been arrested and sentenced to five years in prison.

I braced myself before opening it. I expected despair. Anger. Regret.

Instead, I was met with a tidal wave of gratitude.

He wrote that he was *grateful he got caught,* because it finally stopped the cycle of addiction that was destroying his life. He said prison had given him a second chance—one he wasn't sure he would have taken on his own.

In that moment, my thinking was instantly reframed.

Here I was, silently stewing over my child asking for a second helping of dessert—while Derek, sitting in a cold prison cell, was expressing profound gratitude for his life.

As I walked back into my warm home, with my family safe inside, I felt the weight of perspective settle in. My problems hadn't vanished—but they had been right-sized.

And for that reminder, I was deeply grateful.

In our home, we've made it a practice to share gratitude together as a family. My husband, my kids, and I take a few minutes each day to say what we're grateful for. It's as routine as sitting down for dinner, a small ritual that grounds us.

That doesn't mean it's the only place gratitude lives in my life. I also believe there's enormous value in cultivating community beyond your household.

The only real requirement is willingness.

Choose people who are open, who will show up, and who care enough to participate consistently.

Accountability matters here—not perfection.

Maybe it's a weekly text thread. A monthly gratitude coffee date with a girlfriend. A shared note you update together.

The structure matters less than the commitment.

When we truly connect with those around us, we strengthen our gratitude muscles together. We borrow perspective. We share light. We remind one another what's good when it's hardest to see.

We begin to realize something profound:

Gratitude isn't just a feeling. It's a superpower, especially when we practice it together.

Jessica Janzen's life is a powerful reminder that connection is something we build long before we realize how much we'll need it. Growing up on a farm in Canada, she always craved more energy, more sparkle—and she found it in the fitness world. As a spin instructor and community builder, she discovered something profound: When you look someone in the eye and tell them you believe in them, they begin to believe it too. Through movement, shared energy, and intentional connection, she created spaces where people felt seen, supported, and uplifted. Without realizing it, she was learning a language she would one day rely on in the deepest way.

That language became essential when her son, Lewiston, was diagnosed with Spinal Muscular Atrophy (SMA)—a rare genetic disorder that progressively weakens the muscles and, in its most severe form (Type 1), is often life-limiting in infancy. During the months they had with him, Jessica brought the same spirit of connection into his hospital room—hosting daily dance parties, inviting nurses into moments of joy, and creating light in the darkest of places. And when Lewiston passed, the community she had spent years nurturing showed up for her in return. What she had given so freely came back to hold her.

In the years since, Jessica has turned unimaginable loss into collective purpose—raising millions of dollars, bringing people together, and continuing to lead with joy, generosity, and gratitude.

Her story is a testament to this truth: The connections we cultivate are never wasted.

They are threads we weave over time—threads that, one day, become the net that catches us, the light that guides us, and the strength that carries us forward.

GRATITUDE PAUSE

A Quick-Start Guide to Establishing a Gratitude Community

Sharing one daily reflection with a group can change your relationship with gratitude by creating consistency and accountability. Research from the Greater Good Science Center shows that gratitude practices are more effective when shared socially, amplifying positive emotion and connection (Emmons and McCullough, 2003). The following are three steps for creating your own gratitude community.

1. FORM A SMALL CIRCLE.

Invite two to five individuals—family, friends, or colleagues—who value intentional connection and emotional wellbeing.

2. CREATE A SHARED CHANNEL.

Set up a simple group thread where members can exchange brief gratitude reflections on a daily basis. This can be a text thread, email, Google doc, etc.—whatever is easiest.

3. BUILD THROUGH CONSISTENCY.

Showing up regularly, even if it's only with a shared word or sentence, eventually becomes a habit that over time deepens resilience, fosters meaning, and nurtures a supportive communal rhythm.

Do It Scared

"I experienced a lot of anxiety, but by owning my power, I embraced that this is what I was meant to be doing. By pushing past the fear and being committed to service, I'd come into a place of power."

–Jesse Israel, founder of The Big Quiet

*

"Caitlin is in next. Allison goes in one. Jamie, you're two away."

I heard the ringmaster's voice echo through the loudspeakers at the 1996 Washington International Horse Show, and my entire body went into fight-or-flight. I patted my horse's neck, but my mind was racing. My internal monologue was painfully clear: *I wish I were anywhere but here right now.*

This was the moment I had trained for all year. As a competitive equestrian show jumper, this was *the* competition. You'd think I'd be locked in. Instead, I was locked into fear. The pressure felt suffocating. I remember thinking, fleetingly, that I wished I had never chosen this path at all.

As a junior athlete, I didn't have the luxury of sitting in those thoughts for long. My trainer looked at me and told me—bluntly—to sit up, buck up, and get ready. She reminded me to be grateful. Grateful for the horse beneath me. Grateful for the work we had put in. Grateful for the opportunity to be there at all.

That reminder changed everything.

I urged my horse forward, picked up a canter, and entered the ring. And once I was in motion—once I was fully *in* the moment—the fear fell quiet. Not because it disappeared, but because it no longer mattered. Presence took over.

I won that competition, becoming the youngest rider ever to win the Washington International Horse Show (WIHS) Equitation Finals. But the real prize wasn't the ribbon or the medal. It was the lesson: Showing up scared didn't ruin the moment; it *revealed* it.

One of the great gifts of youth is that we often have coaches, mentors, or authority figures who push us forward when we'd rather retreat. As adults, we don't always have that external voice. We have to become that voice ourselves.

This is where gratitude becomes a powerful ally to courage.

Fear has a way of convincing us to stay small. Every day, we hear stories of people carrying the quiet weight of regret—not because they failed, but because they never tried.

Jesse Israel knows that fear intimately. To him, his fear of failure was crippling. And yet, it didn't disqualify him from his calling—it clarified it. By learning to meet fear head on and choosing service over self-protection, Jesse pushed past his fear—and ultimately landed on a stage with Oprah Winfrey.

Jesse had always felt a little different. He was the kid with the big personality—magnetic, expressive, and often in trouble for it. He had a natural ability to rally people, to stir energy in a room. But alongside that charisma lived a deep undercurrent of anxiety. Even early on, fear showed up loudly in his body, long before he had language for it.

Like many high performers, Jesse became skilled at appearing fine on the outside while quietly unraveling on the inside. As an undergraduate student, he launched a record label out of his dorm room at New York University. The band he signed, MGMT, would go on to become wildly successful. From the outside, it looked like a dream scenario—momentum, access, success.

Inside, the anxiety only intensified.

The more things worked, the more pressure he felt to keep them working.

Success didn't soothe his nervous system; it activated it.

Fear became louder, not quieter. Eventually, something had to give.

That breaking point led Jesse to seek help. He learned a valuable lesson—that raising your hand and saying "I'm not okay" is sometimes the strongest thing we can do. He sought clinical help, through therapy and medication. Things began looking up . . . but he was searching for more. He knew that by taking ownership of the problem, he would feel more in control of the outcome.

That's when he began to explore meditation—not as a lifestyle trend but as a lifeline. Through the practice, he learned how to quiet his mind, regulate his nervous system, and create space between a feeling and a reaction. Over time, what began as personal survival evolved into something much bigger: a desire to share that sense of stillness with others.

That desire became The Big Quiet, a traveling meditation movement that brought moments of collective calm into loud, high-energy spaces. Ironically, the very thing that helped Jesse manage his anxiety eventually placed him in his most anxiety-inducing position yet: standing onstage in front of thousands of people.

When Oprah interviewed Jesse live, she didn't shy away from the irony. She asked him, "How does someone who struggles with anxiety end up speaking onstage at this scale?"

His answer was simple, but profound: "Acceptance."

Jesse doesn't try to eliminate anxiety. He doesn't pretend it's gone. He accepts that it may show up—and he no longer lets that fact dictate his choices. Anxiety, to him, is just a feeling. And a feeling doesn't get to decide the size of his life.

This is where so many of us get stuck.

We believe the goal is to *feel fearless.* To wait until confidence arrives. To act only once discomfort disappears. But acceptance flips that model on its head.

Instead of fighting fear, it teaches us to observe it—without judgment, without panic, without letting it run the show.

When we stop wrestling with anxiety, it loses its grip. Fighting fear often amplifies it. Acceptance, on the other hand, creates distance. We shift from *I am anxious* to *I am noticing anxiety.* That small linguistic change creates perspective.

It reminds us that we are not our feelings—we are people experiencing feelings.

Acceptance also normalizes fear. Anxiety isn't a flaw; it's a protective signal. Like a smoke alarm, it's designed to alert us to perceived danger—not to control our decisions forever.

When we allow discomfort without immediately escaping it, we teach our nervous system something powerful: *I can handle this.*

Over time, fear loosens its hold.

This is the foundation of "doing it scared."

When we reframe a frightening challenge as a privilege—an opportunity to grow, to learn, to test ourselves—our nervous system responds differently. Gratitude helps us zoom out. It reminds us that fear is just one small part of a much bigger universe. Air in our lungs. Ground beneath our feet. A chance to try.

The fear of failure has robbed more people of success than failure ever will.

Often, the real win isn't achieving some prize or desired outcome. It's the pride that comes from showing up despite fear or anxiety. From proving to yourself that fear doesn't get to make your decisions. From building momentum by taking the step—even with shaky knees.

We can be grateful for the chance to fail and learn. Grateful for the opportunity to practice courage. Grateful to simply be alive in a moment that asks something of us.

Jesse mentioned an important reality: The fear may never "go away." It might always tap us on the shoulder before big moments. The gift isn't eliminating it—it's learning to move forward with it riding quietly in the back seat, not gripping the wheel.

Commit to doing big things anyway. Expect fear. Allow it. And proceed.

Because on the other side of doing it scared is pride, growth, and the unmistakable power that comes from choosing not to stay small.

GRATITUDE PAUSE

The "3-3-3" Technique

This grounding technique is commonly used in anxiety-management practices to help bring the mind back to the present. When you find your mind beginning to focus on things beyond your control or getting stuck in one of life's overwhelming moments, this practice helps to reground you by disrupting your anxious thoughts and bringing you back to the present.

This simple meditation strategy encourages you to find presence by recognizing the things you are experiencing in your current environment:

STEP 1: On a piece of paper, write three things you see.

STEP 2: Write three sounds you hear.

STEP 3: Physically touch three things that are near you (these could be external objects or even your own limbs).

How does it work? The "3-3-3" technique forces you to shift your focus from the paralyzing stressors you feel on the inside to the external sensations taking place around you. Through the act of noticing, the practice asks you to be mindful even during a stressful moment and, when achieved, results in a calmer state of mind and a better place to take action.

Enjoy the Present

"All of our lives are a journey of highs and lows. Not everyone's always going to cheer for you. And that's okay. But if you can cheer for yourself and celebrate what is right in front of you, it helps you stand up a little taller. You can't avoid your problems. You might as well tackle them head on."

—Teddi Mellencamp,
podcaster and reality TV star

*

The present moment is the only place where life actually happens—and yet it's the moment we abandon most often.

We spend our days replaying what already happened or rehearsing what might go wrong next. We scroll, we multitask, we cope. And somewhere along the way, joy quietly slips through our fingers. Not because it isn't available, but because we aren't fully there to receive it.

Dark seasons have a way of stealing our joy outright. But even ordinary life can do the same. The relentless pace. The notifications. The mental load. The constant pressure to optimize, improve, and move faster. Over time, we become experts at surviving—but amateurs at savoring. And if gratitude is the practice of noticing what is good, then mindfulness is the discipline of actually staying long enough to feel it.

We live in a world that is always asking us to look elsewhere. This practice is an invitation to return—to gather our attention, bring it home, and fully inhabit the life unfolding in front of us.

Gratitude and mindfulness are often spoken about as separate practices, but in truth, they are inseparable.

Gratitude without presence becomes abstract. Mindfulness without appreciation can feel hollow.

Together, they anchor us, reminding us not only what we are thankful for, but how to experience it fully.

Many of us say we're grateful for our children, our partners, our health, and our lives. And we mean it. But gratitude expressed only in words, without presence in action, has limits. If we're answering emails during dinner, half-listening to bedtime stories while scrolling, or mentally elsewhere during the moments we claim matter most, are we honoring that gratitude, or merely naming it?

Gratitude isn't proven by declaration. It's proven by attention.

Mindfulness asks a simple but uncomfortable question: *Am I actually here for the life I say I'm grateful for?*

I once heard a parable that has stayed with me. A teacher holds up a glass of water and asks her students how heavy it is. Answers vary. "A pound." "Half a pound." She then asks, "What happens if I hold it for a minute?" No problem. "An hour?" The arm starts to ache. "All day?" The pain becomes unbearable. The weight of the glass never changes—but the strain does.

The lesson is clear: It's not the difficulty itself that breaks us; it's how long we carry it without setting it down.

So many of us are holding the glass with one hand . . . while trying to enjoy life with the other.

We're grateful but distracted. Present but preoccupied. Alive but bracing.

This truth becomes painfully clear when time is no longer promised.

When I spoke with Teddi Mellencamp, she shared openly about living most of her life with debilitating anxiety disorders. Anxiety kept her future-focused, hyper-vigilant, and rarely at ease in the present. Much of her energy was spent coping—managing fear, managing symptoms, managing the next shoe waiting to drop. Presence felt elusive, even during moments that should have felt joyful.

And then cancer entered the picture.

When Teddi was diagnosed with melanoma, and later when it spread—first beyond her skin and then to her brain—everything recalibrated. The diagnosis of Stage 4 cancer with four brain tumors didn't just threaten her health.

It stripped away the illusion of endless time. And in that stripping, something sharpened.

When time with her children was no longer assumed, it became sacred. Presence stopped being optional. It became non-negotiable. Teddi began guarding her time—fiercely, instinctively—like the mama bear she is. Distractions lost their power. Noise fell away. What mattered became unmistakably clear. Her cancer didn't eliminate her anxiety, but it allowed her to reprioritize to the point where anxiety was no longer calling all the shots. Not everyone finds clarity in crisis, and there is no "right" way to move through fear or illness. This is just Teddi's experience—one that reshaped her relationship with presence.

This is the cruel paradox of life: So often, we don't fully value the moment until we're afraid of losing it.

We hear this lesson echoed again and again in end-of-life reflections. Hospice nurse Bonnie Ware famously documented the most common regrets of people nearing the end of their lives. Again and again, the same themes emerged: *I wish I'd lived truer to myself. I wish I hadn't worked so much. I wish I'd stayed in touch with friends. I wish I'd allowed myself to be happier.*

Rarely did anyone say, *I wish I'd answered more emails. I wish I'd scrolled more. I wish I'd worried more about things that never happened.*

The regret isn't about lack of achievement. It's about absence of presence.

And here's the invitation embedded in all of this: We don't have to wait for a diagnosis, a crisis, or a wake-up call to start living this way. We can choose it now.

Gratitude brings us back to what matters. Mindfulness keeps us there.

To practice gratitude for the present is to say, *This moment counts.*

To practice mindfulness is to say, *I will show up for it.*

GRATITUDE PAUSE

Guard the Moment

Many of us tumble through the day, errands spilling into activities that then bump into family time before we fall into bed and do it all over again tomorrow. This exercise is about picking one moment to celebrate and then guarding it against distractions, so you are able to be present and cherish the time.

1. FIRST, CHOOSE ONE MOMENT TO GUARD. IT COULD BE:

- A meal
- A conversation
- A walk
- Bedtime
- A quiet morning moment

2. THEN, IDENTIFY THE THINGS THAT TYPICALLY CAUSE DISTRACTIONS. FOR EXAMPLE:

- Scrolling on the phone
- Stress and worry
- Deadlines

- Weak boundaries
- Poor planning

Once you're aware of the distractions, you can engineer the time around this moment to guard against them in the future.

3. MAKE A CONSCIOUS PLAN TO ELIMINATE THESE DISTRACTIONS FROM YOUR GUARDED MOMENT.

- Put your phone in another room or silence notifications.
- Protect the first few minutes of your morning from noise or tasks.
- Let the people around you know you're unavailable for 10 minutes.

4. DECIDE IN ADVANCE: NOTHING ELSE GETS ACCESS TO THIS TIME.

GRATITUDE REMINDER

This moment matters. I am here for it.

Failure Is Fuel

"Gratitude became the one truth. I started focusing on what I wanted instead of what I didn't want. I started saying 'I am' instead of what I wanted people to think I was. Today I'm overflowing . . . and because of that, I'm able to fill other people's cups."

—David Meltzer, speaker, author, and entrepreneur

*

One of the things I think we can all agree on is that none of us likes failure. No one wakes up in the morning thinking, "I hope that client presentation goes terribly today," or, "It would be great if I completely bombed that test." We abhor failure and do whatever we can to avoid it because it can take us off our path, maybe permanently. This is pure survival instinct. We are convinced that, when we fail, we are in an unhealthy place.

But what if failure is a secret ally? I'm not talking about simply learning from mistakes or making lemons out of lemonade here but facing truly daunting challenges and turning them into opportunities to thrive at a higher level than ever before.

Failure can offer chances for growth that simply aren't available any other way.

Failure often requires a response that spurs creative thinking and innovation. You have evidence of what hasn't worked for you, and finding something that *does* work often pushes your thinking in a new way or causes you to look at old things from a new perspective.

Failure can also build resilience. "What doesn't kill you makes you stronger" is a cliché, but the truth is that unless a failure completely takes you out, you come away from it with the knowledge that you've survived and that the consequences of your failure weren't nearly as bad as you feared they might be.

Perhaps the greatest thing to glean from failure is a greater appreciation for what you have.

You might have lost something significant in failing, but what you are left with are things you can be thankful for—things that are permanent and foundational—and things that will help you get on your feet again.

David Meltzer has known an enormous amount of success in his life. He is the co-founder of Sports 1 Marketing, the former CEO of Samsung's smartphone division, and former CEO of Leigh Steinberg Sports & Entertainment Agency, which served as the inspiration for the Hollywood blockbuster *Jerry Maguire*. Today, he's a best-selling author and entrepreneur, the host of the Playbook podcast, and executive producer of the reality business show *Elevator Pitch*.

But he has also known profound failure—something he credits for the life he has today. He'd had a long string of successes—to the point where people were calling him "Midas"—but a lawsuit on a real estate deal put him in need of five million dollars of liquid cash, and when he went to draw down on a line of credit at his bank, he learned that the bank had reduced the limit on all lines of credit to a million dollars, putting him far, far short. In an instant, he was facing the loss of a hundred million dollars and bankruptcy. He was going to lose everything, including the house he'd bought for his mother. The idea of needing to break this news to her nearly broke him. He'd somehow convinced himself that his mother only loved him because of his money and that telling her he was bankrupt and that she was going to suffer for this was going to permanently affect his relationship with her.

Instead, she asked what she could do to help.

This crisis taught him that the people who truly loved him did so because of who he was, not how much he had.

And through this, he found a level of gratitude he'd never known before. This appreciation for the blessings he had and the foundation those blessings provided allowed him to rebuild his business from a much stronger place and to take it in directions he might never have considered if he hadn't failed.

Learning from failure is a lifelong lesson that doesn't only apply to CEOs.

When I was fourteen and in the midst of my horseback riding days, my goal was to compete in one of the major national equitation finals, but I missed qualifying that year by just a couple of points. I was devastated. Instead of letting the failure beat me down or make me question my abilities, I took it as a challenge—one that my very disciplined trainer was happy to oblige! We used the failure as a catalyst to get me rock solid in my foundation. To do this, my trainer first took away my stirrups. As any equestrian knows, your stirrups make riding much easier, and without them you are relying on leg and core strength as well as balance.

Then, one day I showed up to the barn, and not only were my stirrups missing, but my entire saddle was gone. In its place was a bareback pad and a note: "Jamie, see you in the ring." My trainer had hidden my saddle until further notice, which meant I was taking our daily lessons with the other students—only I was riding bareback. I was to tackle the same height jumps and navigate the same highly technical courses as my peers, only without the comfort and stability of a saddle. I understood the challenge to be a gift, not a punishment. And that's exactly what it turned out to be.

Three months later, I learned I had qualified for the finals. Not only did I compete, but I ended up winning that year.

The reason I won was clear: The previous year's failure had lit a fire underneath me to show up in a new way, with a new sense of commitment.

I didn't shy away from the very hard exercises my trainer was putting me through, because I knew that getting solid in my foundation and going the extra mile was ultimately what would set me apart from the crowd. And that's exactly what happened. If I had never failed in the first place, I wouldn't have taken on this new level of commitment. The real win wasn't even the blue ribbon at nationals. It was the pride in learning what I was made of.

Failure is an important element of your gratitude journey.

I've learned to fall in love with my past failures, because they became the fuel that fired me up to work harder and get better.

My failures turned me into a champion.

Not only are failures not inherently "bad," but they can be your strongest life-shapers, boosting you farther ahead as a person than you ever would have been without them. Turn the page for an exercise to help "flip the script" on failure by uncovering the lessons and opportunities for growth that the failure delivered.

GRATITUDE REFLECTION

Failure often requires a response that spurs creative thinking and innovation.

GRATITUDE PAUSE

The Flip-the-Script on Failure Quiz

We all have moments we label as failures—sometimes harshly, sometimes automatically. But failure is rarely the full story. When we slow down and look beneath the surface, these moments often reveal something far more useful: clarity, direction, and the next step forward. This exercise helps you transform a moment of self-criticism into insight and momentum.

Think of one recent moment you labeled as a failure. Complete the prompts below to reframe it with honesty, compassion, and growth.

1. THE FACTS (WHAT ACTUALLY HAPPENED):

Write a brief, judgment-free description of the event. Just the facts—nothing added.

2. THE STORY I ADDED:

What meaning did I attach to it?

(Examples: "I'm not good enough," "I always mess things up," "I should have known better.")

3. WHAT THIS REVEALS:

This moment is showing me something important. What did it highlight about my values, needs, skills, boundaries, or desires?

4. THE OPPORTUNITY HIDDEN INSIDE:

What is one concrete way I could grow, improve, or pivot because of this experience?

5. A GRATITUDE REFRAME:

What can I genuinely appreciate about what this moment taught me?

GRATITUDE REMINDER

Every setback is a signal—pointing me toward the strength, clarity, and growth that are ready to emerge.

Get Knocked Down Once, Get Up Twice

"I very quickly understood that the experience I had been having was curated and imagined as an escape and a fantasy to cope with a very complicated, difficult, and heartbreaking reality that this person existed in. I dare anyone to be confronted with it and not immediately feel compassion."

—Nev Schulman, television host and producer of MTV's *Catfish*

*

In the last chapter, we talked about how failure can fuel both your accomplishments and your sense of gratitude. But what about that very moment when something goes completely and horribly wrong? When it feels as though the rug has been pulled from your life, leaving you lying on the floor and wondering how you can possibly have the fortitude to stand up again? Those experiences, as brutal as they can be to live through, can lead to some of your most powerful breakthroughs, teaching you who you are as a person and inspiring you to not only rise up but stand taller than ever before.

When something doesn't just set you off course but truly knocks you down, it moves you into a level of self-reflection that demands that you take stock of your life. What you find there and what you choose to do with the information has an enormous influence on what comes next.

This isn't just about resilience and recovery. It's about reframing. If you are able to absorb a significant setback, reflect on what it taught you, and make adjustments where you can, you can make yourself stronger in meaningful ways. Sometimes, there's nothing you could have done to prevent a setback, but it's the growth that comes from the setback that helps decide how you move forward.

We all love a great comeback story. I believe we love them because at heart we want to hear about people turning out okay. But we also love them because of the inspiration they generate. We believe that if those people can come back stronger, then we can too.

What great comeback stories tend to have in common is reframing.

When you think about a great comeback, you're likely to realize that the person involved needed to make changes from what they'd always done. I think that's the key lesson here. When you suffer a major setback, if you can reframe your approach—using your innate talents in different ways that address what hasn't worked for you in the past—your chances of thriving after a setback increase dramatically.

Nev Schulman knows all about having the rug pulled out from under him—so much so that he wound up adding a word to the lexicon to describe the experience.

Several years ago, before the word *catfish* became part of our everyday vocabulary, Nev found himself living inside what felt like a modern love story—one that unfolded entirely through screens, texts, and late-night conversations that blurred the line between fantasy and reality.

At the time, Nev was a young filmmaker, creative, curious, and completely captivated by a woman he believed was a stunning, magnetic twenty-something artist living in Michigan. Their connection was electric—flirty messages, intimate conversations, emotional vulnerability—the kind of digital romance that makes you believe you've stumbled into something rare and destined.

There were plans to meet, of course. There always are. And like so many online relationships, those plans kept shifting . . . postponed, rescheduled, wrapped in just enough explanation to keep hope alive. Looking back, the red flags were practically waving in neon lights—but when we're emotionally invested, we often choose possibility over skepticism.

Eventually, curiosity—and maybe a little romantic courage—won out. Nev and his brother packed up and made an unannounced trip to Michigan, expecting to finally meet the woman who had occupied so much of his emotional world.

What he found instead was something entirely different.

The person behind the messages was not the young woman he believed he knew, but a middle-aged woman who had constructed an elaborate digital persona. The connection he thought was real had been carefully manufactured—a reminder of just how easily identity can be shaped, edited, and performed online.

Today, we'd simply say Nev had been "catfished." But back then, the term didn't exist in that context. It was Nev's documentary *Catfish*—and the MTV series that followed—that gave us the language for a phenomenon millions of people now recognize instantly.

The experience was devastating to Nev. He'd invested so much emotionally in this relationship, and he could very well have come away from the experience embittered, furious, and vindictive. Instead, he decided to go a completely different direction. In exchange for her cooperation, he chose not to seek punishment but instead film a documentary that shone a light on the experience from all perspectives so that others could learn from it.

Nev, while being floored by a personal betrayal that could have led him to lose all trust in future relationships, changed course and came back exponentially stronger. His instinct was not to ridicule, save face, or even just walk away. He recognized that behind all the fake profiles was a real person who had a real story. On each and every episode of his show, Nev extends that grace to the people involved. He doesn't assume bad intent, but looks for the humanity, both in the person doing the catfishing and in the person who fell for it.

What Nev gained from his catfishing experience was a heightened sense of gratitude. He told me he feels that it was the best thing that could have happened to him and that it helped to move him to a new and better place.

True gratitude isn't only about being thankful for the good things in your life.

It's also about being grateful for the complicated things—the painful things—because those are the experiences that often activate you.

Sometimes the most traumatic chapters become the turning points.

Nev refers to his catfishing experience as "an essential mistake." It was a misstep that felt humiliating and destabilizing at the time, but in hindsight, it became foundational. Without it, there would be no documentary, no television show, no cultural lexicon built around the word "catfish." What once felt like betrayal became purpose.

Nev's story mirrors my own in a powerful way. What once felt like the worst thing that ever happened to me—my addiction—ultimately revealed itself as an essential mistake. A moment that shattered the illusion I was living inside and forced me to confront who I was and who I needed to become.

Essential mistakes are not gentle teachers.

They don't arrive wrapped in insight. They arrive as chaos. As pain. As the kind of mess you would do almost anything to escape. And yet, they contain lessons that cannot be learned any other way than by walking directly through them.

Had I not fallen into addiction, I would never have discovered how strong I truly was. I would not have learned to embody gratitude the way I do today—because those who have seen the darkest depths see the light that much brighter. When you've lived through a season where tomorrow isn't guaranteed, today stops feeling ordinary. It becomes sacred.

Addiction also showed me what it feels like to live trapped inside yourself—stuck in patterns, beliefs, and behaviors that become a cage of your own making. Breaking free from that cage gave me the tools that now anchor my life: community, spirituality, and service. These aren't concepts I reference casually. They are the pillars that rebuilt me.

Perhaps most importantly, that chapter allowed me to "make my mess my message."

But there's an important caveat: You must teach from the scar, not from the wound.

Healing creates perspective. Perspective creates wisdom. And wisdom is what transforms pain into something useful.

Today, because I've lived both the problem and the solution, I'm equipped to help others do the same. I can tell a story about clawing my way out of addiction on the streets of New York City, and somehow that story resonates with a corporate accountant sitting in a banquet hall in Trumbull, Connecticut. Which is exactly where I found myself last month.

I had just stepped off stage after delivering a keynote to six hundred people packed into a Marriott ballroom. I walked toward the back of the room to hand my mic to the AV tech—that familiar post-keynote moment when a few people hover nearby, waiting to catch your eye.

There's always someone. Someone who needs to say, "That part? That was for me." This time, it was a middle-aged man in a navy suit. He waited until the small crowd cleared and then stepped forward.

“I wasn’t expecting to hear that today,” he said quietly.

“Hear what?” I asked.

“The addiction part. The ‘dark night of the soul’ part.” He swallowed. “I’m not an addict. But I feel like I’m losing myself. And I haven’t told anyone.”

We stood there for a moment in the hum of banquet staff clearing plates.

He went on. “On paper, my life looks great. Good job. Good family. But inside? I feel stuck. And ashamed that I feel stuck.”

I nodded. “That’s the cage,” I said gently. “Different bars. Same cage.”

He let out a breath—the kind that feels like it’s been held for years.

“What if this season,” I asked him, “isn’t the end of your story? What if it’s the chapter that wakes you up?”

His eyes filled. “That’s what I needed to hear,” he said.

When I first began speaking, people would occasionally ask if I worried about sharing my addiction story in front of corporate audiences. Was it appropriate? Would it alienate people? My answer has always been the same: It isn’t just appropriate—it’s essential. Because while not everyone has struggled with addiction, everyone has survived something: loss, heartbreak, betrayal, diagnosis. A season that made them question who they were. An essential mistake.

An essential mistake can harden you, or make you bitter. Or it can become the experience that reshapes your identity and deepens your gratitude. That choice belongs to you. If you lean into the discomfort—if you search for the lesson buried beneath the mud—you may discover that what once felt like your greatest failure becomes your greatest gift. I'm deeply grateful for the essential mistakes along my path. They shaped me. Strengthened me. Clarified me.

What people are truly searching for is proof that there is meaningful, joyful, expansive life on the other side.

Sometimes all it takes is someone holding up a lantern, showing that the path forward still exists.

If you are in a season that feels shaky—worse yet, one that feels like the end—remember this: A bend in the road is not the end of the road, not if you're willing to make the turn.

GRATITUDE PAUSE

Staging Your Comeback

Not all of us need to deal with a situation as dire as Nev Schulman did, but most of us have had situations where we've been thrown off course—where a comeback has been needed. A job loss, a breakup, or something we wish we could undo. Life has a way of surprising us when we least expect it. Sometimes it's small, and other times, it's so big that it feels impossible to come back from. Either way, these setbacks set us off course and make us feel disoriented or unsure how to begin again. This exercise will help you launch your comeback—to help you reclaim your footing and come back stronger.

1. DESCRIBE YOUR SITUATION.

As objectively as possible, write about the circumstances that led to the situation from which you need to come back. Where were you when it all started? What happened? What did it cost you? Try to stick to the facts without judging yourself.

2. IDENTIFY THE LESSON YOU LEARNED.

Every setback teaches us something, even if the lesson is uncomfortable or unexpected. What did the experience of going through this teach you about yourself and about your environment?

3. DISCOVER THE REQUIRED RESET.

Comebacks are rarely possible by repeating the same patterns. Think about what *is* in your control and reflect on what you can change. What needs to change—is it your habits, boundaries, expectations, or support system? What reset is necessary? What steps are required to accomplish this? Focus on adjusting; it doesn't have to be perfect.

4. FEEL GRATITUDE FOR THE OPPORTUNITY.

It can be hard. Sometimes it can even feel impossible to be thankful for a setback. But being grateful is not about liking what happened but noticing what opened up. Did it reveal something important? Redirect you? Strengthen you? What opportunity has this challenge afforded you? Why should you be thankful for it?

5. START YOUR COMEBACK.

Take the first step toward using what you have learned to improve your situation. It doesn't have to be big—think baby steps. Take the first step. And then the next step after that. And then the next. Try to keep each action small, realistic, and grounding. Just remember that a setback may have changed your direction, but the comeback is yours to reclaim.

Help Me.
Thank You.

"You decide your rock bottom. I decided that day in that cell that I was ready to ask for help . . . and accept it. And that's when everything changed."

—Andre Norman, motivational speaker and social change advocate

*

It's 6 a.m. on a Tuesday. The light is streaming through my blinds and hitting me in the face. I squint . . . then jump, as my alarm goes off next to my bed. It's time to wake up . . . which is actually a joke, because I've not yet been to sleep.

I work in public relations, so Tuesday will mean another busy day in my bustling midtown office.

I look around. There are people in my apartment. Some are friends, some I just met the night before. Such is the life of a NYC party girl.

The alarm continues to beep, and I fumble to turn it off. I slowly stand up and get dressed, putting on a grey satin shirt with black pants and high heels. *A costume,* I think. I'm dressing the part of someone who has their life together. But in reality, I'm a mess.

I'm twenty-three years old . . . and I'm an addict.

As I walk toward the subway, listening to the clip-clop of my Manolo Blahniks against the NYC sidewalk, I have a realization—my "white light" moment: *No one is coming to save you. And if you don't ask for help, this will go on forever . . . or at least until something really bad happens.*

I had considered asking for help hundreds of times. I had even picked up the phone and dialed the first few digits of my mother's phone number on at least a dozen occasions. I had a few friends who were on their own recovery journeys too.

So why was I so stuck in reaching out?

For many people, asking for help is the most difficult thing they can do. So many of us have people in our circle who are not only willing to help but would do so happily if they only knew we needed it. Yet we are reluctant to ask. Why is that?

Sadly, many of us equate asking for help with shame. We feel that it is a declaration of weakness, an acknowledgment that we aren't "strong enough" to handle everything ourselves. If we reach out for assistance, we are broadcasting to the world that we are flawed. And on top of this, we feel that reaching out to others puts a huge burden on them, and we don't want to do that to another person. But think about that. If someone you cared about came to you for help, would you feel burdened, or would you feel honored that they asked and pleased to do what you could? My guess is that most people would feel the latter. If that's the case, why wouldn't someone who cared about you feel that way if you were in need?

Well, here's the other reality.

Once you ask for help, you have to actually take action to start fixing the problem. That's right, once you ask for help, you're "on the clock." The moment you go to someone for aid in getting through a difficult situation, you then need to follow through on addressing that situation. And that can be scary. Sometimes having a problem—even a significant one—is easier to deal with than the process of solving that problem.

Asking for help means committing to making a change, and change, even if it is ultimately change for the better, can be unsettling.

We think of an addict's "bottom" as something intense and dramatic. In movies, it often involves the police, a car crash, an overdose. In reality, sometimes it's as simple as having the realization that you're sick and tired of being sick and tired.

For me, that Tuesday morning was the day I decided enough was enough. I stopped at the top of the subway stairs. As people bustled by me, hurriedly bumping into me on their way to work, I fumbled through my bag for my flip phone. I popped it open and called my friend Rex, who I knew was sober. It was time to ask for help.

That day kicked off the next chapter of my life—a new world where I didn't have to walk through my problems alone.

Asking for help changed everything.

Once I got sober, I'd love to say that everything has been easy since then, but that's not reality. In fact, I've had to get honest and ask for help many times since. And each time I've gone through a similar struggle: First I sit in the pain of considering asking for help, then I wait for the problem to either go away (not likely) or blow up (probable). Eventually, the problem gets bigger, and I encounter what I call "the gift of desperation." This is that moment when the pain of the problem gets so big that you are moved to finally take action and bring in the help of others.

Gratitude is a huge factor in all of this. Believe it or not, when I think back on this time, what I'm most grateful for is the pain I was in. That moment when my pain became so great that it compelled me to make a "big girl" decision and ask for help was actually a giant gift, even if it didn't feel that way in the moment. In the moment, it all felt hard and scary. In retrospect, I'm so grateful for the moment of clarity I experienced that Tuesday morning, because it helped me break a cycle of "stuck-ness." By asking for the help I needed, I found the support to break the chains of addiction and find a life of freedom.

Here's the reality: Asking for help is a clear path toward improving your life.

It's unrealistic to think that you can address all your biggest challenges completely on your own. Many of us stall in the process of asking for help because we don't want to "burden" someone else. But the truth is that people often like being asked. It can make them feel special and needed. Humans thrive on helping other humans, so by *not* asking someone to help you, you're actually robbing them of an opportunity to be of service.

Of course, there will be people in the midst of their own battles who may not have the capacity to help—and we want to be sensitive to that. They may be struggling mentally or navigating a crisis of their own. We should approach others with care, but we shouldn't let that awareness turn into self-talk that lets us off the hook.

Even though it may seem bleak in the moment, asking for help is a gratitude amplifier. You get to take a deep breath and receive assistance. You get to learn new skills by inviting in the expertise and guidance of others—whether it's a friend or loved one, a therapist, or a member of a support group like Alcoholics Anonymous (AA). And perhaps most meaningfully, you deepen your relationships by showing up vulnerably and allowing others to meet you with compassion and empathy.

When I interviewed Andre Norman for the podcast, I got a masterclass in the value of asking for help.

Growing up on the tough side of Boston and being put in "the dummy class" (what Andre called the less academically rigorous education track) by schools that didn't recognize his intelligence, he took to a life of crime in his early teens that escalated from assisting drug dealers to *robbing* drug dealers, to home invasion, to felony possession of a firearm, and more. When he was arrested and tried, he wound up with a list of sentences that ran a hundred years. He was eighteen at the time.

Once in prison, he became involved with a gang and then a gang boss. He was shipped to nine different states in an attempt to rehabilitate him, but he wound up with ten more years added to his sentence, including two and a half years in solitary confinement—on top of the hundred years he was serving already.

When he thinks back, Andre admits that he had actually been offered help many times along his path. From the elementary school teacher who saw how smart he was. From the woman who identified his talents as a musician and got him placed in a magnet school. From the man who helped him get into a prestigious international travel program when he was in high school. From the prison counselor who told him about the possibilities of getting his GED and taking college classes. But Andre wasn't in a place where he was ready to truly benefit from that help—until he convinced himself he'd hit rock bottom.

Andre's rock bottom didn't arrive with a dramatic crash. It came quietly, inside those prison walls.

By then, he had climbed high within the prison hierarchy, becoming the second-highest-ranking gang member on the yard. In that world, status offered a form of protection and power. But deep down, Andre knew he wasn't climbing toward freedom—he was just rising inside a cage.

For the first time, he allowed himself to admit that he wanted more. More purpose. More growth. More life than the path he was on could ever offer. And with that realization came another truth: He wouldn't get there alone.

Humility, for many of us, begins with a single moment—the decision to become teachable.

One day, Andre noticed a small group of men gathered together and asked what they were doing. One of them replied by saying they were studying. Without fully understanding why, he felt drawn toward them. He asked if he could study with them.

It was a simple question, but it marked a profound shift—from certainty to curiosity, from survival to growth.

In many ways, it was Andre's first conscious act of gratitude: an acknowledgment that wisdom existed outside himself, and that he was willing to receive it.

The group was led by a man named Natan, whom Andre now describes as a master storyteller. Rather than preaching, Natan shared expansive stories about life, consequence, and humanity. Andre, a practicing Christian, didn't initially realize that Natan was a Rabbi. Titles didn't matter. What he recognized was truth–and a path forward.

Through Natan's mentorship, Andre began learning accountability, responsibility, and servanthood. He learned to examine his choices instead of defending them. He learned that strength wasn't domination but discipline. And perhaps most importantly, he learned that transformation begins when you become grateful enough for a different life that you're willing to be taught how to live it.

According to Andre, Natan taught him how to be human.

And none of it would have happened if he hadn't made the simple decision to ask for–and receive–help. From there, his journey wove through a series of mentors–some religious, some academic, some spiritual–and Andre became fluent in something many of us resist: asking for guidance and allowing it in.

So where did all that asking lead him?

Within eight years, he'd taught himself the law, had his sentence overturned on appeal, and started on a new life. He found a new group of mentors and made it his mission to help others find their right path. Eventually, he was approached by Harvard Law School to participate in their community engagement program. Today, he is a motivational speaker in very high demand and a consultant on corporate social responsibility programs for companies like Delta Airlines, Deutsche Bank, and Major League Baseball. These days, he's referred to as "The Ambassador of Hope."

He has fully embraced the value of receiving help from others and the power that comes from asking. He goes out of his way to help everyone he can. But he makes it very clear: *They* need to find *him*. In other words: *they need to ask*.

His belief is that if someone hears the message, they're already part of a shared connection and they're not alone. The invitation is for them to do their part and respond to that connection and take the next step toward change.

GRATITUDE PAUSE

Gentle Guide to Asking for Help

Asking for help doesn't usually happen in five polished steps. It happens in a moment of honesty—often messy, often emotional, often imperfect. This exercise is designed to meet you there. Think of it as a soft landing, not a checklist.

1. START WITH THE SMALLEST POSSIBLE STEP.

If you're overwhelmed, you don't need a plan. You just need a beginning. Choose one person who feels safe or safe enough—not perfect, not ideal, just safe enough—and send one simple message: "Can we talk?" or "I'm struggling and could use some support." That's it. That counts. This can be a trusted friend, a family member, or a medical professional.

2. YOU DON'T NEED TO KNOW EXACTLY WHAT YOU NEED.

Clarity often comes *after* you reach out, not before. If all you can say is, "Something feels off and I don't know where to start," that is a perfectly valid ask.

3. LET IT BE IMPERFECT.

You don't have to rehearse your words or get them right. You don't have to be composed. You don't have to explain everything. You just have to be honest enough to open the door.

4. RECEIVE THE HELP THAT'S OFFERED.

This might feel uncomfortable—that's normal. Receiving help is a skill, not a personality trait. Let the other person show up for you in the way they naturally can. You don't have to do it gracefully. You just have to stay open.

5. TAKE ONE SMALL NEXT STEP TOGETHER.

Not a full plan. Not a life overhaul. Just the next right thing. Maybe it's scheduling a conversation. Maybe it's asking them to sit with you. Maybe it's letting them help you find additional support. Small steps count. Small steps *are* the work.

1

Impostor Syndrome vs. Inner Hype Man

"I remember sitting in our first board meeting, so freaked out. I didn't know what to say, so I would text my brother/business partner, Michael, under the table a question because I was too intimidated to ask it out loud. He always encouraged me to speak up, and that gave me so much confidence. He would tell me, 'Ya know, we're all here because of you,' and I'd be like, 'Oh yeah, that's right!' That's when I realized you have to own who you are and step into your power."

—Alli Webb, founder of Drybar
and *New York Times* best-selling author

*

Most of us have two voices in our head speaking at the same time—often at different volumes. One is cheering us on, reminding us of our potential, hyping us up like a best friend who knows what we're capable of. The other? That voice is far less kind. It questions whether we belong. Whether we're qualified. Whether we've somehow fooled everyone into thinking we deserve to be here.

That second voice is commonly labeled "impostor syndrome." But here's the reframe: Impostor syndrome isn't a flaw—it's information. It's a signal pointing to parts of us that are outdated, afraid, or overly concerned with external validation.

When we approach impostor syndrome with gratitude instead of resistance, we stop letting it run the show—and start learning from it.

Over years of coaching and personal practice, I've found that impostor syndrome usually shows up as one of three internal archetypes. Each represents a version of you that once served a purpose—but no longer gets to drive.

IMPOSTOR #1: MINI-ME

This is a former version of you—often your inner child—who hasn't caught up with your current growth. Have you ever heard of someone who lost a significant amount of weight but still sees their old body in the mirror? The reality has changed, but the belief hasn't. Mini-Me operates the same way. They remember a time when you felt small, inexperienced, or unsure—and they assume nothing has changed.

Gratitude Reframe: Be the Mentor You Wish You Had

Approach Mini-Me with compassion, not contempt. Thank them for trying to keep you safe from embarrassment or failure. Then remind them—gently but firmly—that you've grown. You've learned. You've earned your place. This isn't dismissal; it's an update. Gratitude allows us to honor where we came from without staying there.

IMPOSTOR #2: LAZY SUSAN

This archetype wants the exit ramp. Lazy Susan is the part of you that labels risk as "too hard" or "too scary" and uses self-doubt as a convenient reason to quit early. If you believe you're not good enough, you won't have to try—and you won't have to risk failing.

Gratitude Reframe: Lean Into Change

With Lazy Susan, a little humor helps. Thank them for highlighting your instinct to retreat—awareness is power. Then reclaim the moment by saying, out loud if possible: "Today, I show up." Growth lives just outside your comfort zone. Gratitude helps us see discomfort not as danger but as an invitation.

IMPOSTOR #3: THE JUDGER

This archetype isn't afraid that you can't succeed—they're afraid of what will happen when you do. The Judger fixates on perception. What will people say? Who will roll their eyes? Will someone try to diminish your win, question your motives, or reduce your success to luck? This voice is deeply uncomfortable with visibility—not because you're unworthy, but because success invites scrutiny.

Gratitude Reframe: Use Judgment as Proof of Expansion
When The Judger shows up, don't thank it for "revealing how much you care." Thank the moment instead. Thank the fact that you are doing something visible enough, bold enough, and meaningful enough to be noticed. Judgment is rarely a sign that you're doing something wrong. More often, it's evidence that you're playing on a bigger field. So when the fear of judgment creeps in, try this reframe: *If someone has an opinion about me, it means I'm visible. If I'm visible, it means I'm growing. And if I'm growing, I'm exactly where I'm meant to be.* You write your story—not the spectators. Be grateful you're brave enough to have one worth talking about.

Here's the fastest way to quiet every version of your inner impostor: Check your intention. Did you step onto that stage to inspire? Start that business to solve a problem? Show up online to connect and serve? Go after that promotion because you bring value?

The moment you shift from "Do I belong?" to "Who can I help?" fear loosens its grip—and faith takes over.

That's Gratitudeology™ in action. When we acknowledge and appreciate the messages behind our self-doubt, they lose their power. Gratitude doesn't silence the inner critic—it reframes it.

If you need proof that impostor syndrome doesn't disqualify you from extraordinary success, look no further than Alli Webb. Alli built Drybar into a cultural phenomenon and sold it for over $255 million—while feeling intimidated, under-credentialed, and unsure she belonged in the room. She didn't wait to feel confident.

"I remember sitting in our first board meeting, so freaked out," she told me. "I didn't know what to say, so I would text my brother under the table a question because I was scared and embarrassed to ask it out loud. He helped give me confidence to be myself. He would tell me, 'Ya know, we're all here because of you,' and I'd be like, 'oh yeah, that's right!' That's when I realized, you have to own who you are."

She learned to own who she was in spite of the fear.

If Alli could build and sell a company of that magnitude while texting questions under the table, what's holding you back?

GRATITUDE PAUSE

Impostor vs. Inner Hype Man Reframes

This practice is about interrupting your inner dialogue in the moment. Impostor syndrome doesn't usually show up as a long speech—it sneaks in as quick thoughts, shaky feelings, or quiet hesitations. The goal here isn't to silence that voice forever. It's to counter it immediately with a stronger, wiser one. Think of this as building a library of ready-made reframes your Inner Hype Man can pull off the shelf when doubt pops up. Below are a few to try on. Borrow them. Tweak them. Make them yours.

REFRAME #1: COMFORT VS. GROWTH

Impostor: This feels uncomfortable.

Inner Hype Man: Growth usually does.

REFRAME #2: FEAR ISN'T A STOP SIGN

Impostor: I'm scared.

Inner Hype Man: Cool. Let's go anyway.

REFRAME #3: NOT KNOWING EVERYTHING

Impostor: I don't know enough yet.

Inner Hype Man: Perfect. Curiosity beats pretending.

REFRAME #4: VISIBILITY ANXIETY

Impostor: People might judge me.

Inner Hype Man: That means I'm doing something worth noticing.

REFRAME #5: COMPARISON SPIRAL

Impostor: Everyone else is ahead of me.

Inner Hype Man: I'm right on time.

REFRAME #6: WAITING TO FEEL READY

Impostor: I should wait until I feel more confident.

Inner Hype Man: Confidence comes after action, not before.

The moment you hear the impostor voice, don't argue with it—reframe it. Say it out loud if you can. Let your Inner Hype Man take the mic and keep you moving.

J

Just. Show. Up.

"Really, really live your life. Have no regrets. Say what you need to say. Be courageous. Be brave. Be bold. Really go every day and just put yourself out there. I'm really grateful for my journey and learning that. If the loss taught me anything, it's that life is short. We just don't know how much time we have. Today, if I want to go for something, I go for it."

—Amanda Kloots, *New York Times* best-selling author, Emmy-nominated host, and wellness founder

*

We've all heard the phrase: *Showing up is half the battle.* But what does "showing up" really mean?

It's not simply being physically present. You and I both know people who are technically there—at work, at dinner, in conversations—but not truly engaged. They're distracted. Disconnected. Phoning it in. And if we're honest, there are moments when we've all done the same.

In a world that feels loud, fast, and endlessly demanding, it's easy to move through life on autopilot—checking boxes, responding to emails, half-watching the moments that are actually meant to matter.

Real showing up is different.

It means bringing your full presence—your energy, attention, and intention—into whatever moment you're standing in. It means choosing engagement over avoidance, curiosity over complacency, and gratitude over numbness.

Sometimes, it takes being shaken awake to remember how precious that choice really is.

For many of us, that awakening arrived in 2020. The world stopped. Certainties dissolved. Routines disappeared. Mortality suddenly felt personal instead of abstract.

At the time, I was living in New York City, juggling motherhood alongside a demanding professional schedule—navigating the daily chaos of Midtown traffic, delayed subway trains, and the very New York reality of schlepping a heavy stroller up endless flights of subway stairs. Then everything changed overnight.

My husband and I made a decision. It was the kind of decision over which we would normally deliberate for months—only this time, we made it within hours. When we heard rumblings of a lockdown, I called my mom and her husband, Jeff. Jeff owns a summer camp in Maine. It's a place where we've spent many happy summers, though I knew their house would be sitting vacant now in the off-season. I launched into my question as soon as they picked up: "Could we hunker down there to ride things out?" Their answer was "yes." It was settled. We packed up our things, tossed our bags in the car, and headed to Maine to ride out the shutdown.

On one hand, it was a wonderful decision—instead of the four of us being crammed into a small New York City apartment, we'd wake up each day to the smell of pine trees, the view of a placid lake, and tons of space for our kiddos to roam. On the other hand, we were even more isolated during a time of mandated isolation.

Like millions of people, we turned to social media for connection. Between balancing work-from-home duties, childcare, and disinfecting groceries, we searched for moments of humanity through tiny screens. And it was there that we—like so many others—became deeply invested in a story unfolding in real time: The story of Amanda Kloots and her husband, Broadway star Nick Cordero.

Before COVID, Nick and Amanda were an entertainment power couple. Nick, a stage actor known for his roles in *Waitress, A Bronx Tale*, and *Bullets Over Broadway*, met Amanda when they were co-starring in a show. He had encouraged her to follow her dreams of building her fitness side-hustle into an empire. They had just welcomed their son Elvis into the world and relocated to Los Angeles when Nick returned from a trip to New York with what seemed like a minor illness—"just a tickle in his throat."

Within days, he was fighting for his life.

As his condition worsened, Amanda turned to social media—first to ask for prayers, and then to create something extraordinary: a daily ritual of collective hope. Every afternoon at 3:00 p.m., she invited the world to play Nick's song, "Live Your Life," and share it online. People across the country—and eventually around the world—filmed themselves belting out the song, often smiling wide, sometimes holding a hairbrush as a makeshift microphone, adding a touch of joy and playful flair to an otherwise heavy moment.

And there we were—my family, in our little hideaway in Maine—belting the song at full volume, invested not just in one man's recovery, but in what his fight represented.

Because watching Amanda show up—day after day, publicly and vulnerably—reminded us of something essential: Life is not a dress rehearsal.

Every single day is an invitation to participate fully—to love loudly, to create boldly, to stop postponing the life we say we want.

Tragically, Nick did not survive. His death became a collective heartbreak–and a powerful wake-up call.

Because "showing up" isn't about simply existing. It's about being awake, alert, and engaged. It's about bringing energy into a room rather than waiting for the room to energize you. Gratitude plays a powerful role here. When you begin to see your life through a lens of appreciation rather than obligation, presence stops feeling heavy and starts feeling meaningful. Responsibilities become opportunities. Moments become gifts.

In the years since, I've watched people redefine how they show up. Friends who once lived only for work now perform in community theater. Others picked up tennis or pickleball simply to celebrate movement and friendship. Some began traveling, no longer waiting for "someday."

For me, showing up meant stepping fully into my purpose–creating the *Gratitudeology™ Podcast* and telling stories like this one. I evaluated my own gifts and realized my role was to be a conduit for inspiration, a container where people could explore gratitude and reimagine their lives through it.

We simply do not know how much time we have. And wasting even one moment disconnected from purpose feels like dishonoring our own lives and those who never got the chance to keep living theirs.

When Amanda later described her grief to me, she compared it to floating in space—suspended, watching life from behind glass. Everything felt distant and surreal. She could have remained there. But she had Elvis. She had to be a mom. She had to show up.

Showing up as a parent reveals something profound: Sometimes the biggest impact happens in the smallest moments.

Your child may not remember whether you watched every second of their favorite movie—but they will remember when you jumped off the couch and sang along with them. Energy creates memory. Memory creates meaning. Not perfection. Presence.

Amanda credits Nick with teaching her what it truly means to live—to say what needs to be said, to be brave, to go for it. And perhaps that is the real lesson of showing up. It's not about being everywhere or doing everything perfectly. It's about choosing presence over postponement. Courage over comfort. Participation over passivity.

Because when you really show up—for your work, your relationships, your purpose—you don't just move through life, you fully experience it.

GRATITUDE REFLECTION

Showing up isn't about doing more. It's about being more present in what you're already doing.

GRATITUDE PAUSE

The Show Up Code

In the moments when "showing up" is a choice, ask yourself: *How do I want to be known for showing up?*

Today, you're going to define your personal **Show Up Code**—a short set of standards for how you choose to engage with your life. This is an exercise to help make "showing up" in small ways a habit for you in your daily life.

STEP 1: REFLECT.

Think about the version of you who is fully engaged, present, and alive. Ask yourself:

- How do I walk into a room?
- How do I listen?
- How do I respond when things feel hard or inconvenient?

STEP 2: CHOOSE YOUR THREE WORDS.

Select three words that define how you want to show up. Examples:

- Present
- Energetic
- Courageous
- Curious
- Playful
- Intentional

STEP 3: PUT YOUR THREE WORDS INTO PRACTICE.

The following day, try to move through the day with those three words as your guide. Before a meeting, a conversation, or even a routine task, pause and ask:

"What would it look like to show up as [your words] right now?"

*If your three words are **Present**, **Courageous**, and **Playful**, here's what that might look like:*

- ***Present:** During a conversation, you put your phone away, make eye contact, and really listen instead of planning your next response.*
- ***Courageous:** In a meeting, you speak up honestly and share an opinion you might normally hold back.*
- ***Playful:** While folding laundry, you turn on music and add a little movement or lightness to the moment.*

STEP 4: CHECK IN.

At the end of the day, ask:

- Where did I live this?
- Where did I default to autopilot?
- What shifted when I was intentional?

Keep returning to your chosen words every day or change them up! The important thing to remember is that you keep showing up. Just remember: These aren't rules; they are reminders for you to be more intentional in your life.

Keep Doing Challenging Things

“We’ve all probably seen that meme where there’s two guys chipping away at a mountain. One stops, the other one does one more chip, and there’s diamonds. That’s life.”

—Clinton Sparks,
Grammy-nominated music producer,
entrepreneur, and visionary

*

There was a season of my life when everything felt uncertain—not because things were falling apart, but because they were pushing me to grow.

In 2015, I was thirty-five years old, newly married to my husband George, and a brand-new mom. George is twenty years older than me, and while he's plugged into the cultural zeitgeist through his job in the music industry, neither of us grew up believing that becoming an "influencer" was a legitimate career path. We were corporate people. He owned a music marketing company. I was a PR executive. Stability mattered.

So when an Instagram account we started—one that documented our life as a fitness-loving couple—began to gain traction, we had a decision to make. At first, it was just fun. We posted about boutique workout classes, wellness routines, healthy recipes, and stories about staying connected as new parents. People resonated. They followed. Engagement grew. And as marketing professionals, we both recognized it: This could be something . . . if we were willing to work for it.

So we became side hustlers.

That meant late nights after bedtime. Long weekends spent building content calendars, shooting and editing videos, pitching collaborations, and learning a platform that was evolving in real time. We were exhausted—and there were no guarantees. For more than a year, we poured ourselves into work that produced little to no financial return.

There were moments we truly questioned our sanity. Were we chasing a pipe dream? Were we too old for this? Were we stealing time from our child for something that might never pay off?

When money did come in, it was modest—a couple hundred dollars per collaboration, barely covering transportation or ingredients for the content we were creating. But we kept showing up anyway.

Why?

Because we believed the true value wasn't the paycheck—it was the contribution.

With every thoughtful post, every class reviewed, every connection made, we knew we were learning, growing, and adding value. And that belief became the fuel.

Then one day, I got a call that changed everything. A PR agency offered me $3,000 to attend an event and post about a product launch. I played it cool on the phone. Hung up. And immediately lost my mind. It wasn't just the money—it was the validation. Someone else finally saw me the way I had already been showing up: as a real creator.

The irony? I was a real creator long before the check arrived. That moment didn't make me legitimate—it confirmed what persistence had already built.

From there, momentum followed. Each benchmark unlocked the next level. Eventually, I would earn five times my corporate salary, build a full-time career as a content creator, and later teach others how to do the same.

People often ask me for the "secret." They want to hack algorithms or copy strategies. But the truth is simpler—and harder.

The reason I succeeded wasn't technical. It was internal.

It was gratitude.

Gratitude kept me patient when results were slow. Gratitude kept me grounded when comparison crept in. Gratitude helped me view effort itself as a win.

Instead of quitting when it was difficult or the results weren't what I wanted, I'd ask: How can I get more creative? How can I make this better? How can I show up one more time?

That's the lesson hidden inside Clinton Sparks's mountain metaphor in this chapter's opening quote. Most people don't fail because they aren't capable. They stop because they assume the diamonds should already be visible. They confuse delay with denial. They mistake difficulty for a sign to turn back.

But growth rarely announces itself. It's built quietly—through one more attempt, one more conversation, one more uncomfortable step.

When gratitude leads the way, challenging things stop feeling like punishment and start feeling like proof that you're expanding.

You don't need certainty to continue. You need conviction.

And that brings us to Clinton Sparks.

Clinton's story is extraordinary—not because it was easy, but because it wasn't. He grew up in Boston with every obstacle imaginable: extreme poverty, an alcoholic father, and experiences of abuse that could have broken his spirit. The cards were stacked firmly against him. But Clinton refused to let this determine his fate. What he did have was ambition—and an unwavering attitude of gratitude.

Instead of asking why me, he asked what's next. He kept showing up. Kept knocking on doors. Kept putting himself in rooms where opportunity lived. That persistence led him from radio DJ to Grammy-nominated producer, collaborating with artists like Lady Gaga and Pitbull, and eventually becoming a multifaceted entrepreneur.

Clinton's success wasn't built overnight. It was chipped away at, patiently, persistently, with faith that something valuable was forming beneath the surface.

That's the invitation here: When life feels hard, it doesn't mean you're doing it wrong. Often, it means you're close.

So keep doing challenging things.

Keep showing up when it would be easier to stop.

Keep believing in work that hasn't paid off yet.

Keep swinging the ax—even when you can't see the diamonds.

Because gratitude doesn't just help you endure the climb.

It helps you trust that the mountain is worth it.

GRATITUDE PAUSE

The "One More Chip" Practice

When progress feels slow, our instinct is to stop—not because we're incapable, but because we can't see what's forming beneath the surface. This practice is designed to help you stay grateful, grounded, and moving forward, even when results aren't visible yet.

STEP 1: NAME THE MOUNTAIN.

What's the goal, project, habit, or dream that's starting to feel heavy?

Right now, I'm working toward ________.

STEP 2: ACKNOWLEDGE THE URGE TO QUIT—WITHOUT JUDGMENT.

Wanting to stop doesn't mean you're weak. It means you're human.

The part of this that feels hardest today is ________.

STEP 3: IDENTIFY YOUR "ONE MORE CHIP."

Identify just one small, doable action you can take today. Not the whole climb. Not the final outcome.

Examples:

- Send one email
- Post one piece of content
- Make one call
- Spend ten focused minutes
- Have the uncomfortable conversation
- *My one more chip today is ________.*

STEP 4: PRACTICE GRATITUDE FOR THE EFFORT—NOT THE RESULT.

Before you do the action, pause and say: I'm grateful for the chance to try again today. This trains your brain to associate progress with participation—not perfection.

STEP 5: RELEASE THE OUTCOME.

You don't need to see the diamonds today.

Your job is simply to keep swinging.

GRATITUDE REMINDER

I don't quit when it's hard. I chip again.

Lean In, Lean Out

“I’m a mom . . . And a business owner . . . And a sister . . . And Jenn . . . And I am the best guide for my children because if I am living a life that I’m ecstatic about and that I love and that I can’t wait to wake up to every day . . . then that gives them permission to do the same.”

–Jenn Drummond, mountaineer and motivational speaker

*

In 2013, a book landed on bookshelves that changed the conversation for working women everywhere. Sheryl Sandberg's *Lean In: Women, Work, and the Will to Lead* challenged women to stop shrinking themselves—to raise their hands, speak up, push harder, and stop apologizing for ambition. At the time, the message felt radical. Empowering. Necessary.

I loved that book.

Like so many women of my generation, I took its message to heart. I leaned in—fully and ferociously—during a period of my life defined by hustle culture and high stakes. I was living in New York City, working in public relations, and climbing the corporate ladder with intensity and pride. I became a Senior Vice President at a major firm, fighting my way toward the top of a competitive industry.

It was exhausting.

It was exhilarating.

And it worked.

Then I had children.

In 2015, I welcomed my first son, Mason, and suddenly the equation changed. The ambition was still there, but so was a new, all-consuming love. I began asking myself new questions like: What does success look like now? Can I be present and powerful? Devoted and driven?

I had long understood that different women's cups are filled by different things—a lesson my mother taught me early. My mom was born in 1950, at a time when the idea of a "working mother" barely existed. Yet she knew from childhood that she was meant to make an impact beyond the walls of her home. It didn't mean she didn't want a family; it meant she wanted family to be part of a bigger life. She used to say to me, "Some women are fulfilled by motherhood alone. Others need motherhood to exist inside a larger dream. Neither is wrong—but self-awareness matters."

She explained that if she had stayed home full-time, a part of her would have felt incomplete, and that would have made her a less present mother, not a better one. Honoring the fullness of her identity allowed her to show up more authentically everywhere.

Growing up, I never resented her demanding schedule as the host of *Good Morning America*. I felt proud. Not just because she was successful, but also because she knew herself well enough to live in alignment.

Looking back, what she was really teaching me was gratitude. She shared with us her struggles—the demanding hours, the constant criticism from the public that any celebrity receives, the challenging personalities inside the TV news ecosystem. She never dismissed these, but it wasn't what she focused on. Instead, she focused on the good. She was grateful for her children. Grateful for her career. Grateful for the awareness to hold space for both.

Because of that example, when I entered my own version of this crossroads, I had a roadmap.

I knew I wanted to continue building my career while embracing motherhood. I shared this journey openly on social media as a wellness and fit-motherhood creator—and the response was . . . complicated. Some messages were supportive. Others were quietly cutting.

"I could never leave my kids with a nanny."

"That must be so hard."

"I feel sorry for you."

Often disguised as concern, the judgment landed heavily. Occasionally, it was overt—full-blown mom-shaming from strangers who felt entitled to weigh in on choices they knew nothing about. It baffled me. Motherhood is already vulnerable terrain. Why make it harder for one another?

But here's what anchored me: gratitude.

I am deeply grateful for my boys—and I am equally certain of my purpose in this world. I believe I am here to make an impact and leave a legacy. That calling requires commitment, courage, and yes, work. Gratitude allowed me to hold both truths without guilt.

I've since learned that this tension—the pull between "leaning in" and "leaning out"—isn't a flaw. It's an invitation. Because fulfillment doesn't come from choosing one identity over another. It comes from honoring the truth of what fills your cup.

That truth became strikingly clear in the story of another woman who faced this same reckoning. Author, athlete, and motivational speaker Jenn Drummond is the mother of seven children. After leaving a successful career in finance, she stepped fully into stay-at-home motherhood, believing she was doing what she should want. For a time, she tried to convince herself it was enough.

Then came the Thanksgiving party at her kids' school.

Standing in a classroom decorated with turkeys, wearing a feathered hair scrunchie someone had kindly handed her, preparing to run bingo with the PTA moms, Jenn felt something inside her crack. Not because the moment was wrong—but because it didn't feel right for her.

She slipped into the bathroom, fighting back tears, and asked herself a question that many women silently carry: *How did I end up here, and is this really the life I want?*

For some women, that moment would have felt joyful and fulfilling. For Jenn, it felt hollow. Not because she didn't love her children, but because something essential was missing. That awareness wasn't selfish. It was honest.

And honesty changed everything.

After surviving a near-fatal car accident that forced her to confront her mortality, Jenn decided she would no longer ignore the quiet voice asking for more.

She leaned back into herself—into challenge, growth, and possibility.

She went on to become the first woman—and only the second human—to climb the Seven Second Summits, the second-highest peaks on every continent. Today, she's a sought-after speaker and coach who teaches women to live boldly, intentionally, and without apology.

Jenn's story isn't about climbing mountains.

It's about listening when your soul whispers that you're meant for expansion.

She didn't lean out of motherhood. She leaned into herself.

And that is what this is really about.

"Lean In, Lean Out" isn't a directive—it's a discernment. There will be seasons to push forward. Seasons to pull back. Seasons to do both simultaneously. Gratitude gives us the clarity to know which season we're in—and the confidence to honor it without shame.

Because when we stop living by someone else's definition of fulfillment and start living in alignment with our own, we don't abandon our responsibilities.

We elevate them.

And that—more than any book or movement—is how women build lives that feel whole.

GRATITUDE PAUSE

Lean In or Lean Out?

Knowing when to lean in and when to lean out is deeply situational. There is no universal formula for fulfillment—only awareness, informed by your season of life, your responsibilities, and your capacity. This exercise will help you get honest about where you are right now.

ASK YOURSELF:

- What is filling my cup right now?
- What is draining it?
- Am I honoring this season . . . or fighting it?

THEN CHOOSE ONE SENTENCE TO COMPLETE:

In this season of my life, I'm allowed to lean ________.
(in, out, back, forward—or simply into myself)

GRATITUDE REMINDER

Alignment is not selfish. It's how I show up as my best self.

Moonshots and Manifestations

"I don't know how I got here . . . well, yes I do. It was sixteen or seventeen years of non-stop working. There is no secret to it. It was a lot of work to get here. I just set the vision, and then I kept my head down, and I worked."

—Chloe Melas,
entertainment journalist

*

Chloe Melas and I came up in the same era—the early 2000s—when work culture looked very different than it does today.

It was louder. Sharper. More competitive. There were toxic bosses, bruised egos, and plenty of moments that could have convinced you to quit if you were looking for a reason. Back then, there were no wellness seminars or conversations about psychological safety. You either developed thick skin, or you were eaten alive.

And yet, those of us who had a clear vision of where we wanted to go used those challenges as fuel. We didn't interpret criticism as personal failure. We treated it as information. We didn't see rejection as a stop sign. We saw it as a detour. We kept our eyes on the prize and learned to metabolize discomfort as part of the journey.

That's where moonshots—actions that move you toward your "shoot for the moon" goals—come in.

When people talk about manifestation, it can sometimes sound mystical—like wishful thinking or magical optimism. But manifestation, at its core, is something much simpler and far more grounded.

It's the act of holding a vision so clearly, and with so much belief, that your behavior naturally aligns with it.

You think about it.

You feel gratitude for it before it exists.

You act as if it's possible.

And over time, that energy compounds.

There's a pointed difference between the mindset that fixates on what could go wrong and the one that's willing to imagine what could go right.

Sometimes people get trapped in the loop of asking: *What if it doesn't work out?* That thought breeds fear, hesitation, and paralysis.

Manifestors ask a different question: *What if it does?*

They are willing to hold gratitude for success that hasn't happened yet, and that mindset opens doors.

I've always joked that one of my greatest assets is a healthy dose of delusion—a deep, internal belief that everything will work out. *The world is conspiring in my favor.* It sounds silly until you realize that nearly every thought leader who teaches manifestation asks you to practice exactly that. These aren't empty affirmations; they're cognitive training tools.

And the good news? This way of thinking isn't something you're born with. It's trainable.

What if I fail? This is an entirely reasonable question to ask whenever you're out of your comfort zone. But when that question is asked with courage instead of fear, it makes the difference between a life lived expansively and one lived cautiously in the shadows.

I learned this early in my career.

From the time I was a kid, I knew I wanted to work in public relations. It was all about who you knew back then, and my entry point came through a chance encounter that could have gone very differently.

I was nineteen years old, freelancing as an on-the-ground reporter at the Hampton Classic horse show. In the middle of interviewing a high-profile rider, a well-known New York City PR maven—the kind who "ran the city"—tried to barge in to grab a photo.

I told her to back off.

She stormed away.

Only later did I learn who she was.

I had two options: Shrink in embarrassment or take the shot.

I chose the shot.

I marched into the VIP tent, introduced myself, and said I thought we'd gotten off on the wrong foot. She laughed, told me she liked my sass, and when I mentioned I was looking for an internship in New York, she said, "Be in my office Monday."

That internship placed me at the center of New York society and culture—movie premieres, fashion events, and celebrity chaos.

It was also brutal.

Most days, I knew I'd be yelled at. Think *The Devil Wears Prada,* but worse. My mother, who had broken her own glass ceilings, told me, "If you have to cry, do it quietly in the bathroom. Then get back to your desk."

Wild. Unacceptable today. But formative.

One night, I was working the door at a movie premiere, clipboard in hand, when Regis Philbin walked up. He recognized me—he'd worked with my mom for years—and immediately understood where I was employed. He leaned in and said, "Jamie, this is baptism by fire. If you can survive this, you can do anything."

He was right. That job taught me my first major life lesson: Take shots. Don't back down because something is hard. Hard often means you're standing in the right room.

With each role that followed, I gained evidence. Evidence that big swings lead to big growth. Sometimes financially. Sometimes emotionally. Always developmentally.

I could have walked away bitter. I could have created a narrative that women tear each other down, or that the industry wasn't for me. Instead, I chose gratitude.

Gratitude for resilience.

Gratitude for access.

Gratitude for learning how to survive any environment.

That perspective shaped everything that followed, including how I manifest today.

When I launched my *Gratitudeology™ Podcast*, people often asked how I landed such high-profile guests. The truth? I asked, and I never assumed they'd say no. I believed in the mission. I believed in myself. And that belief carried an energy that attracted yes after yes—including Chloe's.

When I asked Chloe to join me, I knew her career climb was impressive. What I didn't fully grasp at the time was how much life had tested her along the way.

Just when Chloe had reached her dream, working on air at NBC, married, raising two young boys, disaster struck. A fire that began in her chimney burned down her home.

In an instant, everything changed.

She could have chosen the narrative that life always knocks her down. Instead, she chose gratitude. The fire restored her faith in humanity. It reminded her that people matter more than things. And it strengthened her resolve to rebuild—for her family and herself.

That resilience became fuel.

Shortly after, Chloe took another moonshot: applying for her role at NBC—the *TODAY* show, the pinnacle she'd envisioned for years.

"To walk into 30 Rock is a pinch-me moment," she told me. "I walk around with a permanent smile on my face. You'll see Jimmy Fallon or Seth Meyers. You'll bump into Hoda or Al Roker or Savannah—it's a dream."

When I asked her the secret to reaching a dream most people only fantasize about, she brought it back to basics.

"I don't know how I got here . . . well, yes I do. It was sixteen or seventeen years of nonstop working. There's no secret. I set the vision, kept my head down, and worked."

That's the truth about moonshots.

They aren't magic and they aren't instant.

They are built rung by rung, fueled by belief, gratitude, and the willingness to keep showing up.

You set the vision.

You hold the faith.

You take the shot.

And one day, you look up and realize: You flew.

GRATITUDE PAUSE

Your Moonshot Script

A moonshot isn't a reckless dream. It's the goal that feels slightly unreasonable, but deeply aligned. Scripting is an exercise that will help you identify your personal moonshot and begin calling it into existence. The idea behind scripting is that by visualizing your future and putting it on paper in the present tense, you're already living in that reality. Take a breath. Grab a pen. Let's begin.

STEP 1: NAME IT.

What goal keeps resurfacing in your mind, even when you try to ignore it?

- A career move
- A creative pursuit
- A lifestyle shift
- A financial goal
- A version of yourself you keep imagining

That's your moonshot.

STEP 2: SCRIPT IT.

Write about it as if it has already happened. Use present tense—not "I will," but "I am."

Try this:

I am so grateful that my moonshot is now my reality.

My life looks like ________.

I feel ________ every day.

This version of me shows up with ________.

Add detail. Add emotion. Feel the gratitude.

STEP 3: LET IT GO—THEN MOVE ON.

Once you've written your script:

- Read it once more
- Close the notebook
- Let go of when or how it will happen

ASK YOURSELF:

What is one small action I can take this week that aligns with this vision?

GRATITUDE REMINDER

When you feel grateful for what hasn't happened yet, you teach your mind to expect possibility and align your frequency to receive it.

Now Is When

"If today was my last day, could I look back on my life without any regret? I'd never taken the time to look at my life through that perspective. And I just realized instantly: 'Oh my God . . . I'd change everything.'"

—Seb Terry, best-selling author and top keynote speaker

*

A few years ago, I was walking down the sidewalk in New York City, hand in hand with my husband, George . . . and I began to cry.

He looked at me quizzically, then asked the obvious question: "What's wrong?"

Here's the tough part. My answer was, "Nothing . . . really."

I watched his face contort into that special brand of confusion only a cryptic wife can incite in her loving husband, so I dug deeper to expand on the answer.

"I was just thinking . . . wondering, really, I suppose," I stammered. "Have you ever felt like you were on a professional high, but a spiritual low . . . at the exact same time?"

He looked at me and nodded. "I think everyone feels that way sometimes."

George was absolutely right.

It is incredibly common to feel disconnected and unsatisfied—even while checking all the boxes you once believed would make you happy.

What I was feeling wasn't failure. It wasn't even burnout. It was yearning. A quiet but persistent pull toward something more alive.

I realized I had been so focused on ambition—on doing all the things I thought I was "supposed to do"—that I had forgotten to actually *live*. Travel had become a someday plan. Adventure felt indulgent. Risk-taking seemed irresponsible. Whimsy, spirituality, long walks in nature, spontaneous memory-making—all of it had been gently pushed aside in service of productivity.

And eventually, that kind of postponement collects interest.

What I was experiencing wasn't a lack of success. It was a hunger for presence.

I had been building a life—I just hadn't been fully inside it.

It wasn't that I was lacking gratitude. I was deeply aware of my blessings, and I spent real time acknowledging them: a strong marriage, motherhood, professional success, and a life that looked, from the outside, full and meaningful. But I began to realize something important—something many of us quietly wrestle with but rarely say out loud: Being grateful isn't the same thing as being satisfied.

And it's okay to seek satisfaction; in fact, it's imperative.

Gratitude roots us in appreciation for what already exists, but it doesn't erase the pull toward growth, exploration, or expansion. In fact, that pull is often a sign of gratitude itself—a desire to fully experience the life we've been given. Yet many of us live in what I think of as "wait mode," holding our dreams at arm's length while we wait for some "magical" future moment that will somehow be more convenient or more appropriate.

How often do you daydream about that next meaningful step you'd like to take? Even if you feel that you are in a very good place, there are likely dreams still on the table. Maybe it's traveling someplace you've never been. Maybe it's learning a new skill or a new language. Maybe it's getting the certification you need to level up at work. Maybe it's turning Friday night into date night. We're talking about dreams of all scales and all levels of attainability.

Now, when considering those dreams, how often do you follow with, "I'll do that when . . . ?" *I'll do it when my schedule opens up. When the kids are older. When I have a little more money. When . . . the time is right.* You probably have excellent reasons for forestalling your next goal. Good sense often dictates that we stay the course.

But let's look at a contradiction that is equally true on both sides.

The time is never right.

It's unlikely that you're sitting around with your feet up whiling away the hours. Our personal time is like the space in our homes: No matter how much you have, you can fill up all of it. Yes, you have countless responsibilities, demands from others, and a to-do list as long as your arm. Meanwhile, your resources are never as many as you would like them to be. You don't have enough people to cover for you in a pinch. Your bank balance isn't high enough. You're already working ten hours a day and you're already not getting enough sleep. There literally aren't enough hours in the day.

So if we're waiting for ideal conditions, we may end up waiting indefinitely.

This was the realization I began circling back to during that season of yearning:

If the moment is never perfectly convenient, then perhaps the question isn't whether now is ideal—but whether now is enough.

Again, just do the math. If it's *always* a bad time, then *now* is as good as *ever.* Does that seem impractical? Maybe. But if you really want something, there's only one way to get it. And when you start to work toward that new goal, there's an extremely good chance that the practical impediments will start to fall away. It's a bit like having room for dessert after a big meal, and there aren't even any extra calories involved. If it's something you want, and it's something you know you'll enjoy, it'll be delicious.

Seb Terry knows all about not waiting until tomorrow to pursue your dreams. He told me that for him it started when a close friend of his died at age twenty-four. Seb said he asked himself whether his friend would have had any regrets for the time he'd been given, and he didn't think he would have. But he then wondered how he would have felt in the same situation—and realized he would have changed everything.

Realizing he wasn't happy, he asked himself what he needed to do. And he decided to make a list.

Seb wound up writing down a hundred things that he hoped would propel him toward a sense of happiness and purpose in his life. And then he set about to accomplish those things. Big things, little things, surprising things. Once he realized the power of finding greater purpose and joy by pushing himself to experience unexpected things, he turned his personal journey into more, which is when it grew into a global movement. Today, Seb is still working on his list (he's checked off seventy-seven of the hundred as of this writing), and he has become an internationally renowned keynote speaker and best-selling author.

You don't need to compile a list of a hundred things you want to do before you die. Start with five. Start with one.

What's important is that you stop putting off your dreams and start acting on them now.

GRATITUDE REFLECTION

Gratitude roots us in appreciation for what already exists, but it doesn't erase the pull toward growth, exploration, or expansion.

GRATITUDE PAUSE

Getting Your Dreams Off the Starting Line

We often have very good reasons for putting off our goals. Adding the pursuit of a dream to your already busy day is a bit like trying to fit a new piece of furniture—let's say a bookshelf—into an already crowded room. How, exactly, are you going to accomplish that?

Of course, this exercise only makes sense if you absolutely want the "bookshelf." That's a conversation you need to have with yourself before you even begin.

STEP 1: LOOK AROUND THE ROOM.

Bookshelves take up a fair amount of space, and every inch of your room is being used. Where is the bookshelf going to fit?

Take a quick audit of your available time and how much time the pursuit of your dream is going to fill up. Is there any empty space in there?

STEP 2: START MOVING STUFF OUT.

A lot of the stuff in this room has been here for a long time. I don't even remember when I got that thing.

Are you spending time during your day on things that are no longer worth it? Ask yourself, "If I stopped doing ______, would it make any difference to me or anyone I loved?" If the answer is no, it's probably time to stop doing that thing.

STEP 3: START MOVING STUFF AROUND.

Now that I've moved out the ______, the bookshelf could probably fit in that corner. But I'm still going to need to shift around a few pieces of furniture.

In addition to the things you can stop doing, there are probably one or two things that you could do more efficiently. How can you spend less time on some of your everyday responsibilities? Are there other things you can do less frequently than you do them now?

STEP 4: BRING IN THE BOOKSHELF.

I've cleared the space, now let's put the bookshelf there. Looks great, doesn't it?

You've given yourself the freedom to pursue a new dream. Celebrate it and enjoy how great your room looks now.

GRATITUDE REMINDER

If I really want it, I can find a way to pursue it.

O

Only Way Out Is Through

“One of the things I was born with was discernment. Discernment is an understanding of knowing what it is I’m supposed to be doing. So I don’t know what the future is going to look like, but my discernment is telling me where I need to go, and whatever comes, I’ll figure it out.”

—Lizzie Ens, author of *Amish Renegade*, influencer, podcaster, and holistic wellness practitioner

*

Think of some of the scariest things you've ever done. Maybe it was asking someone on a date. Maybe it was telling your boss you're taking another job. Maybe it was strapping on skis for the first time and pointing yourself down a mountain. What made those things so scary? *I could be humiliated. I could disappoint someone. I could wind up in the hospital.* All very legitimate concerns and all very possible outcomes.

But then think about why you found yourself in this position in the first place. *I really like this person. The new job is just too good to turn down. People tell me skiing is a thrill ride.* There's only one way to get to the good stuff, and the path runs right through the scary stuff.

The truth is that the path to what we want almost always runs straight through what we fear.

Sometimes things go badly. But more often than not, even when it's awkward or uncomfortable, we come out the other side stronger—either having attained the thing we were after or at least with proof that we were brave enough to try.

And when we choose not to act? When fear wins? We stay exactly where we are.

Hard things are hard because they stretch us. They demand growth before we feel ready. But the reward isn't just the outcome—it's who we become in the process.

There are no shortcuts. The only way out is through.

In the last chapter, we talked about how easy it is to sell yourself on the notion that the time isn't right for a new endeavor. Hopefully, you've now convinced yourself that this method of thinking only leaves you with lots of unfulfilled goals. But even if you've gotten past that point, you might still face another issue: What you want to accomplish can be daunting.

Lizzie Ens grew up in one of the more densely populated and strictest Amish towns in Ohio. As you probably know, among the Amish, modern conveniences that you and I take for granted—like electricity, computers and cars—are forbidden because they believe that those things weaken the bonds of family and community. After years of living in the Amish culture, Lizzie got to a point where she felt trapped.

And she knew she had to do something about it.

So one fateful day, she waited until her entire family had finished supper, and she pretended she was going up to her room on the second floor to go to sleep. Then she opened her bedroom window and crawled up on the roof. After thirty minutes of weighing the consequences of leaving against the certainty of an unfulfilled life, she jumped. It turned out to be the best decision she possibly could have made.

Lizzie Ens lives a life that includes multiple entrepreneurial successes, a popular podcast, a book, and millions of social media followers. And she attributes a great deal of what she's accomplished to gratitude for providing her with the hope and healing she needed to live so boldly.

How many of us have had our own roof moment? A moment when we knew—deep down—that if we didn't jump, we would stay stuck forever.

Mine didn't involve shingles or a second-story drop. But it did involve fear so thick I could taste it.

When I was deep in addiction, I must have dialed half of my mother's phone number fifty times. I'd get as far as the fourth or fifth digit, then hang up. My heart would pound. My mind would spiral. What if she was disappointed? What if I couldn't fix this? What if saying it out loud made it real?

But here's the thing about rock bottom: Pretending you're not there doesn't move you off it.

The night I finally made the call—when I finally told the truth—was my jump off the roof. It didn't feel triumphant. It felt terrifying. But it was the only way into recovery, into healing, into the version of my life I live today.

I've stood on other roofs since then. I've stood at the base of five-foot show-jumping fences, staring at rails that looked impossibly high, wanting nothing more than to circle away and quit. I've stood in marathon training at mile eighteen, legs shaking, lungs burning, wishing there were some magical detour that could transport me to the finish line without the suffering in between.

There wasn't. There never is.

In riding, you can't win the ribbon without taking the jump.

In marathon training, you can't show up to the starting line unless you've logged the miles. In recovery, you can't get free without first getting honest.

Every meaningful transformation in my life required the same thing: walking directly into the discomfort instead of negotiating with it.

That's what Lizzie did on that roof. She let go of the version of herself that was bound by fear and stepped into uncertainty. She didn't know what the future would look like—but her discernment told her she had to move.

And that's the quiet miracle of going through something hard.

When you stop trying to escape the discomfort and instead decide to endure it, something shifts. You stop being a victim of circumstance and start becoming the author of your own next chapter.

Yes, sometimes it hurts. Yes, sometimes you fall.

But on the other side of "through" is almost always freedom.

GRATITUDE PAUSE

Making a Bold Move

Most of us have a goal that we know would improve our lives but that requires some possibly scary steps to accomplish. This exercise gives you a template for contemplating that challenge.

STEP 1: IDENTIFY AN UNEXPLORED GOAL.

What is something you've contemplated achieving but set aside?

I know in my heart that I should ________.

STEP 2: NAME WHAT'S STOPPING YOU.

Put your fears out there. Acknowledge the worst-case scenarios.

If I fail, then________.

STEP 3: CONTEMPLATE THE BENEFITS.

Dig deep into how your life would improve if you succeeded.

If this goes the right way, I could ________.

STEP 4: TAKE THE FIRST TINY STEP.

If you're convinced that the benefits outweigh the risks, determine what you can do to take the first step toward your goal—and then do it.

The right time is a myth. Bold moves are rarely made from a place of certainty—they're made by people willing to act before they feel fully ready.

So take the step. One day you'll look back and realize the thing that changed everything wasn't a perfect plan—it was a single courageous move.

Protect Your Energy

"I just know that when we are selfish, that's when we go down. When we're only thinking about ourselves, that's when our minds start to play these really dark tricks on us. Take all that energy and put it into action. For me, that saved my life."

–Caroline D'Amore, CEO of Pizza Girl and media personality

*

Of all the self-help advice offered—meditate more, say no, wake up earlier, drink more water—protecting your energy might be the most important of all.

Because your energy is the one thing that is solely yours to guard.

No one else can manage it for you. No one can protect it on your behalf. It's an inside job, and if you don't learn how to tend to it, life can feel unbearably heavy.

I learned that lesson much earlier than most.

It was a muggy summer day in Rye, the New York City suburb where I grew up. I was twelve years old, and my cotton sundress was sticking to my sweaty back as I stared at something that felt . . . wrong.

The hinges on our screen door are gone. Not broken. Not loose. Removed.

There's a uniquely violating feeling when you realize someone outside your family has messed with your home. But this wasn't about stealing something tangible like money or jewelry. Whoever did this was searching for information.

Dirt.

My parents were in the midst of a divorce—already painful, already disorienting. But my family's situation carried another layer entirely. My mother's role as co-host of *Good Morning America* meant she shared each of her three pregnancies with the world. She had built her brand around being "America's mom."

So when the divorce began, the public wanted details. And tabloids—ruthless and unchecked in that era—were willing to manufacture them.

Photographers followed us to horse shows, deliberately trying to spook my mother's horse so they could capture a fall. A decoy once approached my father's car under the guise of asking for directions, only for the tabloids to later label the staged photo as him soliciting a prostitute.

And now, someone had removed the hinges from our door to snoop. We immediately suspected it was a nosy reporter, a fact which was later confirmed.

At twelve years old, life is already confusing enough. Add public scrutiny and predatory adults, and it's overwhelming.

I had a choice, though I didn't know it then. I could absorb the chaos. Decide the world was cruel. Carry fear, anger, or mistrust into adulthood. Or I could learn—slowly, imperfectly—how to protect my energy.

My saving grace was my mother, who even in the midst of the chaos, expertly modeled this behavior.

At the very moment her own life was being shaken up, I was watching her learn to protect her energy instead of getting caught in the tornado or turmoil. She had every right to be angry, bitter, and resentful, but she refused to let these things take root.

Instead, she taught us one central truth:

The only thing we truly control is how we show up.

Our behavior.

Our beliefs.

Our energy.

Looking back, I realize something profound:

There will always be someone trying to pull at your hinges, trying to burst into your space through a "loose screen door."

People who manipulate for gain.

People acting from unhealed wounds.

People who thrive on chaos.

They don't disappear with adulthood; they just change form.

I met them again years later—this time as a mother.

"Mom, can I talk to you?"

My son Mason stood in front of me, tears welling in his eyes. He and his younger brother were being bullied on the bus. He had tried to handle it himself, but it kept escalating between him and the other boy until it became too big for him to manage alone.

That's when he turned to me.

My instinct was to fix it. I reached out to the other parents, expecting a calm conversation. Maybe we'd bring the kids together. Teach accountability. Model resolution.

That's not what happened. Instead, things escalated quickly. Sharp text messages. Defensiveness. Accusations. Hostility.

It felt familiar. Once again, someone was yanking at my hinges, trying to barge in and steal my peace.

They felt like the type of people who thrive on the adrenaline rush of conflict. It's easy to get sucked in. As a mother, it's easy to feel the instinct to defend your kids. To protect, to advocate, to prove your point.

And just like when I was twelve, it felt unfair. I felt self-righteous anger. I wanted to win. To prove that they were the bad guys. To feel vindication.

But I remembered what my mother had taught me all those years ago:

Engaging with chaos doesn't create clarity. It just pulls you into someone else's bad vibration.

So I paused and asked myself one essential question: What matters more–being right, or protecting my energy?

The answer changed everything.

I made three conscious choices:

- **I disengaged from the emotional argument.**
- **I redirected my focus toward keeping my children safe.**
- **And I re-centered on what I could control: my energy.**

It didn't mean the situation disappeared overnight. They're our neighbors, so unfortunately, we still felt the discomfort. But the heaviness lifted the moment I stopped feeding it.

Here's what that experience reminded me:

- **Not every conflict deserves your participation.**
- **Not every explanation requires your energy.**
- **Not every open door needs to stay open.**
- **Sometimes peace is the bravest choice.**

The hinge metaphor followed me full circle—from a twelve-year-old girl watching adults violate her home, to a grown woman realizing that emotional boundaries are just as sacred as physical ones. That's why protecting your energy matters so deeply.

And it's also why Caroline D'Amore's story resonates so powerfully.

Caroline has endured profound loss—the early death of her mother, a near-death struggle with addiction, and betrayal by a notorious conman. Again and again, life challenged her resilience.

What she discovered is simple but powerful: When we collapse inward, pain echoes louder; when we direct our energy toward purpose and service, we transform suffering into strength.

When the devastating Pacific Palisades fires burned through Caroline's hometown, she stood at a crossroads familiar to anyone who has faced sudden loss: retreat into helplessness or rise into action.

She chose to rise.

Caroline is also known as "Pizza Girl," a name she acquired as the owner of two popular restaurants and a retail business built around cute (pink!) pizza equipment and accessories.

Instead of collapsing into fear, she converted shock into service, loading up a caravan of vans with hot pizzas and committing to feeding frontline workers fighting the fires.

Movement became her medicine. Action became her gratitude in motion—not as denial of the pain but as transformation of it.

Caroline doesn't deny pain. She simply refuses to let it dominate. That is what protecting your energy really looks like.

It isn't avoidance.

It isn't pretending everything is fine.

It's choosing where your life force goes—and where it doesn't.

So the question becomes: Who and what do you allow to pull at your hinges?

When you stop giving energy to every situation, you don't become closed off. You become intentional—opening only where growth lives and closing where peace is protected.

GRATITUDE PAUSE

Lion's Breath: Reclaim Your Energy

When your energy feels scattered, heavy, or hijacked by emotion, Lion's Breath is a powerful way to reset your nervous system and reclaim your life force. Used in yoga to harness prana—your vital energy—this breath helps release tension, anger, and overwhelm.

HOW TO PRACTICE:

Step 1: Sit comfortably or kneel, spine tall.

Step 2: Inhale deeply through your nose.

Step 3: Open your mouth wide, stick out your tongue, and exhale forcefully with a strong "HA" sound.

Step 4: Let your eyes widen and your jaw relax.

Repeat three to five times.

As you exhale, imagine releasing anything that has been pulling at your hinges.

GRATITUDE REMINDER

Your energy is sacred. You get to decide who—and what—has access to it.

Quiet the Mind

"When you are more present, you become a better version of yourself. You become more attractive. You attract more abundance into your life"

—Light Watkins, best-selling author, global speaker, and mindfulness expert

*

Most people think gratitude is only something you *do*—a list you write, a mindset you practice, a reminder you set on your phone.

But gratitude isn't something you chase.

It's something you notice.

And noticing requires one thing most of us struggle to access in a world that never stops moving: presence.

Not the Instagram version of presence. Not the "take a deep breath and carry on" version. Real presence—the kind where your mind quiets enough to let life unfold in front of you without rushing past it.

But, as we've discussed elsewhere, being present is *hard.* Distractions are everywhere, and even if you can condition yourself to step away from your screens and devices for a few hours every day, there's enough distraction clanging around in your mind to make being fully present a Herculean challenge.

My relationship with meditation has been . . . complicated.

I'm a child of the '90s, which means I grew up watching all the cool alternative people lean into yoga, incense, and Eastern philosophy long before it became mainstream. I devoured the *Tao Te Ching* mostly because it felt mysterious and wise, read cult-favorite books like *The Tao of Pooh* and *The Te of Piglet*, and watched characters on *Absolutely Fabulous* trot off to meditation retreats as if enlightenment were the ultimate form of chic rebellion. I loved the *idea* of meditation. I just wasn't particularly good at doing it.

Over the years, I tried—truly. I would sit down with the best intentions, close my eyes, and attempt to "quiet my mind," only to discover that my brain had absolutely no interest in cooperating. Instead of blissful silence, I got grocery lists, awkward conversations from 2007, and a running commentary about whether I should reorganize my closet.

It wasn't until treatment for addiction that meditation began to make practical sense. Suddenly, it wasn't framed as something mystical or inaccessible—it became a tool. Grounding exercises like naming five things you see, five things you hear, and five things you feel gave my busy brain something tangible to focus on. That shifted everything. Meditation didn't have to look one specific way; it could have entry points, structure, rhythm.

Years later, when boutique meditation studios started popping up across New York City, I found myself attending because—if I'm honest—they were extremely Instagrammable. There were beautiful crystals, mushroom coffees, and retail spaces that felt like curated dreamscapes. I'd show up, soak in the vibe, maybe attempt the practice—and often leave thinking, "Well, that was lovely . . . and also very hard."

Which is part of the reason meditation can feel intimidating. Many people assume they're doing it wrong if their minds wander or if they don't instantly achieve some transcendent state. That assumption keeps a lot of us from fully engaging with a practice that is, at its core, remarkably simple.

Quieting your mind isn't about eliminating thoughts or forcing silence. It's about creating space—even briefly—between the noise.

Even a short period of intentional stillness can function like an emotional reset. Thoughts that felt tangled begin to organize themselves. Focus sharpens. The nervous system gets a moment to exhale. Research increasingly supports what meditation practitioners have known for centuries: Regular mindfulness practices can reduce stress and anxiety, improve memory and attention, enhance sleep quality, and help regulate emotional responses. It's less about escaping life and more about returning to it with clarity.

So why doesn't everyone meditate?

For some, it still feels fringe or "too woo-woo." For others, it feels inaccessible–something reserved for monks or people who naturally possess a quiet mind. I've spoken with countless people who say, "I tried to meditate, but I can't do it." And honestly, I used to feel the same way.

That perspective began to change when I met Light Watkins.

I first encountered Light at a high-level professional development gathering for keynote speakers–the kind of event where introductions sound like résumé highlights. During cocktail hour, I shook hands with people who casually described themselves as "the former mayor of San Diego" or "the guy who invented

Spotify," and I felt wildly intimidated. So when I saw an incredibly tall and handsome man walking across the room, I assumed he was yet another larger-than-life personality whose shadow I'd spend the evening trying not to hide in.

But when he introduced himself, something felt different.

His energy was grounded in a way that felt almost otherworldly—quiet, warm, completely free of the subtle ego performance that often fills rooms like that. His eyes sparkled with calm amusement, and there was a gentle upturn to his mouth that wasn't quite a smirk—more like a reflection of someone who understood something about the chaos of life that the rest of us were still trying to figure out.

That was Light Watkins.

Light is a longtime meditation teacher and thought leader who has spoken and consulted at Fortune 500 companies around the world on mindfulness, purpose, and enlightened leadership. He is the author of multiple best-selling books and has coached a wide range of high-profile clients, including Rosario Dawson, Jonah Hill, and Meghan Markle. But more than any credential, what struck me was how fully he embodied the principles he taught. Being around him felt like standing next to a walking meditation.

In our conversations, Light explained meditation in a way that immediately made it feel more accessible, likening it to the experience of doing something, like listening to a podcast, and suddenly realizing that twenty minutes have passed and you don't recall what happened—something we all have done.

That reframing changed everything for me.

Meditation wasn't about forcing stillness; it was about recognizing a state I already knew—and learning how to access it intentionally.

Light also acknowledges that for many of us raised in the Western world, meditation can feel clunky at first but that if we stick to it, it begins to flow. He describes meditation as a release valve for accumulated stress–a way of allowing the body and mind to reset in a world that rarely slows down. Perhaps that's why practices resembling meditation have existed for thousands of years across cultures and traditions. They endure because they work.

And yet, one of the greatest lessons I've learned is that meditation doesn't have to look the same for everyone.

These days, as a working mother juggling a thousand moving pieces, guided meditation sometimes turns into what I jokingly call an "expensive nap." And honestly? I'm okay with that. Over time, I've discovered that moving meditations–long runs, especially the half marathon length–are where my mind quiets most naturally. There's something about the rhythm of breath and movement that creates an unexpected stillness. For two hours, there is nothing to solve, nowhere else to be, no competing demands. Just presence.

That realization changed how I think about meditation entirely. Maybe the goal isn't to force ourselves into a single definition of mindfulness, but to recognize the moments where presence already exists—and lean into them.

Perhaps that gentle half-smile I noticed when I first met Light was rooted in this understanding. We spend so much time worrying about whether we're "doing it right," when the deeper truth is that the doorway to stillness has always been available to us.

Over time, Light took this philosophy even further. He became nomadic while writing his book *Traveling Light*, living untethered—carrying only what he truly needed. Watching him do that felt radical in the most peaceful way. It wasn't about escape. It was about intention. About not letting possessions, expectations, or mental clutter dictate the terms of your life.

Years ago, when I moved from New York City to Los Angeles, I did something similar. I sold nearly everything I owned and packed what remained into my little silver Volkswagen Beetle. Everything that mattered—or so I believed—fit inside that car. There was something wildly liberating about that moment. Not because minimalism is morally superior, but because shedding the excess forced clarity. What do I actually need? What is just noise?

That, to me, is the deeper invitation of quieting your mind.

Not necessarily to sell all your belongings or become nomadic—though you could—but to untether yourself from the mental minutiae that weighs you down. The replayed arguments. The imagined catastrophes. The endless comparison. The identity clutter.

What would it feel like to move through your days carrying only what you need?

To travel light—not just physically but mentally?

When you quiet your mind, you begin to realize how much of what you're carrying isn't required. And when you put some of it down—even briefly—gratitude has room to breathe. Because beneath the noise, beneath the striving, beneath the clutter . . . your life is already enough.

And when you learn to return to that truth—again and again—you don't just quiet your mind.

You free it.

GRATITUDE PAUSE

Meditation for Beginners

Here's a quick-start meditation guide for beginners.

STEP 1: FIND A QUIET, RELAXING SPACE.

Seek out someplace where you can get comfortable, either sitting or lying down, and where you'll be free from outside distractions.

STEP 2: CLOSE YOUR EYES AND CONCENTRATE ON YOUR BREATHING.

Focusing on your breathing will help center you and will be a useful tool in keeping your thoughts at bay. Many people choose to use a mantra—a repeated sound that has no external meaning—for the same purpose.

STEP 3: DON'T FIGHT THE THOUGHTS; JUST SET THEM ASIDE.

One of the reasons people feel they aren't capable of meditating is because they believe they are failing if any thoughts enter their minds. That's not the case at all. Instead, when thoughts enter, train yourself to push them away until later, while you return to your mantra or your focus on breathing.

STEP 4: START SMALL AND BUILD FROM THERE.

Light and many others recommend meditating for twenty minutes. However, that might seem like an eternity to you at first. Try starting with five minutes and building from there.

Relationship Reflection

“Never settle for a partner who doesn’t push you to grow, who doesn’t match your energy, and who doesn’t share your ambition.”

–Dr. Nadine Macaluso, trauma bond expert, author, and real-life ex-wife of the “Wolf of Wall Street”

*

"Why don't you have a boyfriend?"

My friend Tracy tossed the question casually as we walked down a street in the East Village.

"Because I'm happy!" I shot back, playfully. "And I'm not looking for anyone to mess that up."

Tracy Young–Grammy-winning music producer, DJ, and longtime friend–knew me from my nightlife days. She'd seen me at my worst and cheered me back to life after I stepped away from New York City to enter addiction treatment. That particular evening, I was supporting her on the red carpet in my role as her publicist.

Her question was harmless, but for me, it unearthed a deeper truth.

For most of my romantic life up to that point, I had chosen partners who matched the chaotic energy I once carried. Fiery. Unreliable. Damaged. I didn't understand back then that our relationships tend to mirror our internal state.

But by the time I was walking with Tracy that night, I had changed. I had spent years in therapy and personal development work. I had peeled back old wounds, challenged outdated patterns, and learned how to be alone without feeling lonely. I was happy. Fulfilled. And deeply grateful.

Gratitude had become my North Star.

In that new reality, the idea of inviting someone potentially toxic into my life–someone who might disrupt my peace–felt almost laughable. What I didn't yet realize was something important: Doing the inner work doesn't just heal you. It prepares you to attract a different kind of partner.

I've always loved the saying that relationships aren't 50/50—they're 100/100. It means we're not looking for someone to complete us. That's a recipe for codependence. Instead, we're meant to become whole on our own and then choose someone who complements that wholeness.

When two full people come together, they don't drain each other. They expand.

That night, Tracy insisted on setting me up with her friend George. "He works in music, he's grounded, you'll love him," she said.

What could one blind date hurt?

That date changed my life.

George and I didn't just fall in love—we built a shared philosophy. From the beginning, we decided that gratitude would be the centerpiece of our relationship.

We both had pasts that could have broken us: addiction, painful relationships, and experiences that might have hardened us. Instead of carrying those stories forward as baggage, we chose to anchor our partnership in gratitude—for who we were becoming, for what we were building, and for what was right in front of us.

We started humbly—a tiny studio apartment, two people committed to being grateful for the life they were creating together. Today, our life is big and beautiful. But we say this all the time: If tomorrow all the "cash and prizes" disappeared, we'd still be okay.

Because gratitude is our rock.

This kind of gratitude isn't poetic or passive. It's practical. It's intentional. Every day presents the typical stress—exhaustion, schedules, small irritations, moments where it's easy to forget how lucky we are.

The difference is that we actively pull ourselves back to gratitude. Together.

We pray. We read. We check in with one another. We start each school morning with our boys sharing what they're grateful for: "Daddy tying my shoes." "Mommy making pancakes." "Our home."

That daily practice isn't just sweet, it's relational glue.

And science backs this up.

A dissertation study by Erica Pearse Ragan at University of Denver titled "Thank You, Dear: Examining the Association Between Gratitude and Relationship Well-Being" found that gratitude doesn't just make couples feel better, it actively protects and strengthens relationships. Gratitude helps partners rediscover positive feelings for one another and build emotional reserves that allow them to better weather stress and adversity. In fact, the research suggests that many relationships don't end because of explosive conflict; rather, they simply fade when partners "grow apart." Gratitude can help reverse that drift by rebuilding connection and appreciation.

Simply put, this is emotional infrastructure that can be the difference between a relationship that survives and one that thrives.

If you believe in the Law of Attraction (and I do!), you'll agree with me on this: One of the greatest benefits of a gratitude-centered relationship is that it exists on a higher vibrational frequency. What does that mean? In practical terms, gratitude shifts your attention toward what's working rather than what's missing, and that shift changes how you show up, how you interpret challenges, and ultimately what you attract into your shared experience.

When two people consistently focus on appreciation instead of deficiency, they create momentum, and momentum has a way of pulling more good into its orbit.

I've always believed that you and your partner should make each other the best version of yourselves—not just emotionally but creatively, professionally, and spiritually. George and I realized early on that we weren't just life partners—we wanted to be teammates.

I've seen so many relationships where, once the chemistry wears off, there's not much left.

But when you're truly grateful to be woven into the fabric of someone's life, when you admire how they think, how they build, and how they dream, the relationship doesn't rely solely on sparks.

It doesn't mean that everything is easy. Like any spiritual exercise, gratitude takes daily practice. We view the practice of gratitude as a daily discipline. We say, "thank you." We notice effort. We apologize quickly. We choose appreciation—especially on the hard days.

Now, I know talking about a "great relationship" can make some people roll their eyes. And I get it. Not everyone is in a partnership, and not every partnership is healthy.

Let's be clear: Gratitude can't fix everything. If someone doesn't value you, cheats, disrespects your boundaries, or consistently undermines your worth, gratitude will not save that relationship. Those situations require courage, clarity, and sometimes walking away.

This is where Dr. Nadine Macaluso's voice becomes essential.

In her twenties, Nadine was swept into what looked like a fairy tale—a glamorous life with a charismatic, wildly successful man:

Jordan Belfort, the real-life "Wolf of Wall Street." What began as intoxicating love and luxury quickly revealed a darker undercurrent. The intensity that once felt thrilling became destabilizing, pulling her further away from herself.

Nothing illustrates this more clearly than the yacht named after her: *The Nadine*. A floating symbol of excess, the 167-foot (51 m) luxury vessel embodied the lavish lifestyle and grand gestures that defined their relationship. But during a violent storm off the coast of Sardinia, the yacht sank, nearly taking their lives with it.

In many ways, the moment mirrored Nadine's own journey. What once appeared glamorous was, underneath, deeply unsafe. Her gratitude had been misplaced, directed toward status, wealth, and spectacle rather than toward alignment, safety, and self-respect. Only when she reclaimed gratitude for herself, her children, and the life she wanted to model for them did she find the strength to leave, rebuild, and begin again.

Today Nadine—also known as "Dr. Nae" to her hundreds of thousands of followers on social media—is a licensed psychotherapist and author who helps people recognize relational trauma and narcissistic abuse.

She notes that gratitude isn't about being thankful for everything but rather being thankful for the right things.

That distinction changes everything.

Choosing the right partner is half the work. Depending on who you pick, that person can be an arsonist or an architect.

But once you've found your person, everything changes.

Gratitude turns love from a feeling into a practice—one that strengthens connection, softens conflict, and fuels growth.

Love stops being something you hope will last and becomes something you intentionally build.

And that is how two whole people create a partnership that doesn't just survive but thrives beyond their wildest dreams.

GRATITUDE PAUSE

The Naikan Reflection (A Buddhist Practice for Deeper Gratitude)

Naikan is a Japanese contemplative practice rooted in Buddhism. It simply means "looking inward." Instead of focusing only on what we receive, Naikan invites balance, humility, and clarity through three questions:

- *What have I received from my partner?*
- *What have I given to my partner?*
- *What difficulties have I caused my partner?*

This isn't about blame—it's about awareness.

HOW TO TRY IT TONIGHT:

Sit quietly (alone or together). Reflect honestly on the three questions. If practicing as a couple, take turns sharing—beginning with what you've received.

Naikan shifts relationships from scorekeeping to gratitude—and from defensiveness to growth.

Superpowers and Self-Promotion

"I speak onstage amidst a lot of powerful male speakers, and I used to let it psych me out. Now, the one thing to say before I get onstage is 'Be more Jen.' Because the only thing that makes me unique and different is the special thing that only I bring to the table."

—Jen Gottlieb, best-selling author and sought-after keynote speaker

*

Let me tell you something that might make you uncomfortable.

You are wildly underestimating yourself.

Not because you lack talent. Not because you haven't earned your seat. But because you've normalized your own magic.

We all have superpowers—not the cinematic kind but the deeply human kind. The kind that lives in the space between what feels natural to us and what feels nearly impossible to someone else. The problem is that we dismiss them. We call them "just something I do." We assume everyone else can do it too.

They can't.

Jen Gottlieb knew from a young age that she was meant to perform. Some people discover their superpower accidentally; Jen sensed hers early. She played Annie when she was ten years old and felt something click. The stage didn't scare her. It energized her. It felt like home.

But here's what I love most about her story: She didn't wait for Broadway to validate that instinct.

As she was growing into herself, she allowed her superpower to evolve in less obvious places. She worked at Hooters. And when I asked her on the podcast what that experience felt like, she didn't flinch or downplay it.

She practically shouted: "I loved it!"

Not because of the uniform or the tips, but because it was a stage. She loved making people smile. She loved turning an ordinary interaction into something memorable. The restaurant became a training ground. The world was her rehearsal space. She wasn't waiting for the "right" platform; she was strengthening her gift wherever she stood.

That's what people who understand their superpowers do. They practice them. They refine them. They look for arenas, not approval.

By the time Jen stepped into Broadway and later onto MTV as a host, she wasn't discovering her presence—she had been cultivating it for years. And when that chapter ended, she didn't panic. She recognized that what powered her performance career wasn't just talent; it was visibility, magnetism, and connection. So she built a company around it. She codified it. She taught it. She became known for it—co-founding Super Connector Media, authoring *Be Seen,* and stepping onto keynote stages alongside some of the most recognizable voices in the world.

Before she walks on stage now, instead of spiraling about who she should emulate, she simply tells herself, "Be Jen. Be more Jen."

That line is deceptively simple. It isn't about becoming louder or flashier. It's about becoming more aligned with what is already uniquely yours.

Watching Jen own that so unapologetically forced me to examine my own blind spots. What personal superpowers was I hiding, fighting, or mislabeling?

For years, I carried impostor syndrome around negotiation. Negotiating felt aggressive to me—sharp-elbowed and intimidating—something "real businesspeople" did. Meanwhile, I kept finding myself in conversations where partnerships came together naturally. Creative collaborations. Experiential campaigns. Multi-layered programs where every party walked away energized rather than squeezed. I told myself it was chemistry. Or timing. Or luck.

It wasn't.

What I eventually recognized was that I wasn't negotiating through dominance; I was negotiating through alignment.

I love thinking through value from multiple angles. I over-prepare. I anticipate objections. I build trust quickly because I genuinely enjoy the people on the other end of the phone. Once there is trust, agreement follows more easily.

Those weren't personality quirks. They were strengths I hadn't named.

And that's how superpowers often operate. They hide in plain sight. They sit inside the things we already do well until a moment—or a mirror—forces us to see them clearly.

A friend discovered she was an extraordinary organizer while downsizing her home, approaching the move like a logic puzzle and navigating it with unexpected mastery. That skill had always been there, but it took a shift in environment to reveal it.

Many of our superpowers work this way. A parent managing the logistics of a school fundraiser may be exercising high-level project management and negotiation skills. A friend who consistently mediates conflict may possess rare emotional intelligence and diplomatic strength. Once you separate the skill from the setting, you begin to see its transferability.

The lesson in all of these stories isn't "be impressive." It's this: Your superpower may not look glamorous at first. It may show up in unexpected arenas. It may even hide behind something you once dismissed. But if it energizes you and creates value for others, it is worth naming.

And once you name it, you are responsible for using it.

This is where self-promotion enters the conversation. Many people become uncomfortable at the idea of promoting themselves. It feels boastful. Ego-driven. Like stepping too far into the light. Yet if you have a superpower and you refuse to let it be seen, you are not practicing humility; you are practicing concealment.

True self-promotion is not shouting your accolades into the void. It is making people aware of how you can serve them. It is clarity about what you do well and confidence in offering it.

When rooted in gratitude rather than ego, self-promotion becomes stewardship.

And while it may feel uncomfortable to step forward, hiding your strengths does not make you humbler—it simply keeps your impact smaller than it could be.

If you believe your abilities are blessings, then using them fully is not arrogance; it is alignment.

Superpowers are not meant to be hidden out of politeness. They are meant to be refined, strengthened, and shared.

Gratitude asks us to acknowledge the blessings in our lives—not only the obvious ones, like love and opportunity, but also the strengths we carry.

Yet many of us overlook the gifts that sit closest to us because they feel ordinary.

They aren't ordinary. They are invitations.

The moment you begin to own your superpowers publicly, vulnerability follows. Visibility invites scrutiny, and not everyone will understand your confidence. This is often the point when individuals retreat, convincing themselves that staying small is safer.

But diminishing your brilliance does not make you more likable. It simply makes you less impactful.

Gratitude at its highest level is active. It asks you not only to acknowledge what you have been given but to build around it.

When you recognize your superpower and allow it to be visible, you create pathways for service, opportunity, and growth.

The world does not benefit from your hesitation nearly as much as it benefits from your clarity.

So instead of obsessing over where you fall short, examine where you excel. Notice what energizes you. Pay attention to the patterns in what people consistently seek you out for. Name those strengths without flinching and then build your life around them.

Your superpowers are not accidents. They are assignments.

And once you recognize them, the question is no longer whether you are capable. The question is whether you are willing to be seen using them.

GRATITUDE PAUSE

Audit Your Superpowers

Most people don't lack talent—they lack recognition. We normalize what comes naturally to us and assume it isn't special because we assume these things come naturally to everyone. This exercise will help you identify the things about you that are truly special, things that most people can't do as well as you and that others admire your ability to do.

ASK YOURSELF:

- *What feels intuitive to me but difficult to others?*
- *What do people consistently compliment me on or ask me for help with?*
- *What leaves me energized instead of drained?*

Patterns are evidence.

Now consider: *Where am I minimizing this strength? Am I downplaying it because naming it feels boastful?*

Finish this sentence without hedging:
"My superpower is _____."

You cannot steward what you refuse to acknowledge. Name it clearly—not for applause but for impact. When you acknowledge your unique abilities, you're expressing an appreciation for them by appreciating what is already within you, honoring the people and experiences that shaped you, and choosing to use them instead of hiding them.

Temper the Terror

"The actual moment of doing it, whether it's a tough conversation or whether it's going out on stage, there's a tidal wave moment where, yeah, you're in it. If you can just hang in there and just stand there and even breathe for a second, it's not going to be that intense for that long. And then there's this moment of beautiful peace on the other side."

—Lori Harder, entrepreneur and podcast host

*

We all know the feeling. Our heart rate soars. Our breathing quickens. Our muscles tense. Our stomach clenches. Our skin crawls. We sweat. We feel hot and cold at the same time. We might even have trouble staying on our feet.

Fear is not fun.

And it's not just physical—fear can hijack your thoughts, shrink your courage, and convince you to stay small. Sometimes the anticipation of fear becomes its own form of paralysis.

Here's the truth: Fear will always exist. If you're living fully, you will encounter moments that make you uncomfortable—whether it's stepping onto a stage, changing careers, or simply raising your hand and saying, "I want more."

But fear doesn't have to debilitate you. In fact, it can become one of your greatest tools.

Fear exists to protect us. Those adrenaline-fueled responses once helped humans survive saber-toothed tigers. Today, they still signal something important: What we're doing matters. Performers often say that if they don't feel nervous before going on stage, something is wrong. Fear isn't proof that you're unprepared—it's proof that you care.

And when you learn to temper the terror instead of running from it, you unlock something powerful.

Lori Harder knows this firsthand. Growing up in a tiny community and being raised in a highly religious, restrictive home, she had no idea of her capabilities, and she was filled with doubts. At a personal development workshop, participants were invited to share openly into a microphone—her worst nightmare. Fighting back her fear, she managed to stand at the mic—but instead of speaking, she started crying.

The facilitator told her that she was in a safe space and that, whenever she was ready, the room wanted to hear what she had to say. She managed to share her fears with the group, lived through the experience, and realized that she now had proof that she could manage an incredibly difficult situation.

What Lori learned in that moment was that fear is a temporary thing, and if you can get past it, the fear is replaced by a powerful sense of freedom—a freedom that comes with knowing you're going to get to the other side.

Lori likens fear to a surfer facing an enormous wave. The wave looks terrifying as it approaches, but once you ride it, the water settles.

And I know this is true because I've lived it.

I'll never forget a moment in my own life that was riddled with terror—though looking back now, it's almost comical.

The year was 2019. I had just left my full-time job as an executive at a PR agency, leaning into my "Act Two" as a content creator and wellness personality. I had become popular on social media as a fitness influencer, and my work with brands as a paid ambassador had begun to transcend social media and push me toward television.

To be clear, I had dabbled in some light TV gigs. I had appeared on local news as a wellness expert a few times and even had a brief stint on a national talk show on behalf of a laxative medication—helping Americans "close their fiber gap" (a.k.a. poop). I wouldn't say I had exactly "made it," but I was on my way-ish.

Leaving my corporate job was already terrifying. I had been a public relations executive for nearly two decades, earning a multi-six-figure salary with benefits, and when I gave notice, I was walking away from stability for the dream of becoming an entrepreneur and building my personal brand.

Oh—and did I mention I was six months pregnant at the time?

I gave my notice despite the fear because I believed in myself enough to know it was time to leap and trust the net would appear.

Then, shortly after giving birth via emergency C-section, my phone rang while I was sitting in my New York City apartment.

"Jamie," my agent said carefully, "could you get to QVC in Pennsylvania on Tuesday? They want to audition you as an on-air ambassador."

I looked down at my healing body—swollen, stitched, wrapped in hospital-issued underwear—and said the only thing I could: "Sure."

Days later, I pulled into the QVC parking lot at 7 a.m., having done glam at 3 a.m. and driven through the night. Sitting alone in my car before walking inside, I faced two immediate tasks: rehearsing my talking points . . . and using my breast pump.

Yes—there I was, shirt off in the backseat, practicing lines while being milked like a cow before the most important audition of my life.

Ten out of ten. Highly recommend.

I joke now, but in that moment, I was spiraling. Fear hit hard. Impostor syndrome roared. Who was I to do this? I was a new mom, exhausted, vulnerable, unsure.

Not to mention, this was for a sleek athleisure brand. I was swollen, lactating, and still bleeding. I wasn't even sure I was up for the job under the best of circumstances—but today? TODAY?

But as we've already established, rock-bottom moments offer clarity. I had two options: Drive home, or step forward.

I decided it was a good time for affirmations.

"You've . . . got this," I squeaked out timidly.

I cleared my throat.

"You've got this, and you're freakin' amazing."

Better.

"And you're powerful. And beautiful. And smart. AND FUNNY!"

I was yelling now.

"And you're a mother-flippin' new mom who got herself out the door and glammed up at 3 a.m. because you are a human who can do hard things—and YOU CAN DO THIS!"

To this day, I wonder if anyone in the adjacent cars noticed a half-nude woman with bouncy curls screaming motivational mantras at herself in the backseat of a Ford Explorer.

By the time I finished—both pumping and pep-talking—I was ready.

I packed my bags (both my slim work bag and my breast pump bag, which absolutely had to come with me unless I wanted to resemble Dolly Parton by lunchtime), tidied myself up, and walked through the double glass doors into the impressive lobby.

As I signed in with security, I smiled to myself.

You're going to get this job.

And guess what? I did.

I've been on the air at QVC for the past seven years, and I am eternally grateful to the version of myself who showed up that day. I'm also grateful for the fear—okay, the terror—because it taught me something important.

Fear, I've learned, is a phenomenal motivator.

It drove me to prepare relentlessly, to study harder, to show up sharper. And yes, I was terrified of succeeding too—of being judged by a national audience. But without stepping into that fear, I never would have experienced the joy waiting on the other side.

That's the thing about fear: It guards the doorway to expansion.

Seven years later, I can trace so many beautiful moments back to that morning: growth, friendships, new opportunities, even the relocation to Pennsylvania that reshaped my family's life.

All because I chose to temper the terror instead of surrender to it.

Courage rarely arrives as confidence. More often, it looks messy—exhausted, uncertain, maybe half-dressed in a parking lot before dawn.

Courage isn't the absence of fear; it's the decision to move anyway.

When you walk toward fear, it changes shape. It becomes momentum. It becomes proof of growth.

Tempering the terror isn't about becoming fearless.

It's about becoming someone who knows she can walk forward anyway.

GRATITUDE PAUSE

How to Temper the Terror in Real Time

Next time fear hits before a big moment—a presentation, a hard conversation, a leap—don't try to eliminate it. Do this instead:

STEP 1: NAME THE FEAR.

Say it out loud. "I'm afraid I'll fail." "I'm afraid I'll look stupid." Fear shrinks when it's spoken.

STEP 2: CREATE YOUR PROOF.

Ask yourself: *When have I done something hard before and come out fine on the other side?* Lock in one memory. That's your reference point.

STEP 3: CONVINCE YOURSELF—AND SAY YOUR TRUTH LIKE YOU MEAN IT.

Out loud. In your car. In the mirror. Wherever.

"I've got this."

"I can do hard things."

"Yes, I'm terrified. And yes, I'm going anyway."

STEP 4: WALK THROUGH THE DOOR.

Not after the fear goes away. While it's still there.
Because courage isn't the absence of terror.
It's movement in spite of it.

Unearth Your Purpose

“Man, if I spent my whole life doing this, it feels like trying to empty the ocean with an eyedropper . . . It’s so big and I’m so small—would it even matter?

—Justin Wren, founder of Fight for the Forgotten

*

When I launched the *Gratitudeology™ Podcast*, I had two immediate goals.

The goal for the first episode would be to tell my story—my journey through addiction—because I wanted listeners to understand why gratitude had become my mission.

The goal for the second episode? To interview Justin Wren.

Justin embodies something rare: mission-driven gratitude. The kind that isn't performative or poetic but lived, tested, and forged through real hardship.

When you first meet Justin, you see the fighter. Massive frame. Tattoos. A red beard that makes him look like a Viking who wandered into a meditation retreat. But sit with him long enough and you feel something else entirely—deep presence, quiet humility, and a profound sense of purpose.

Justin's early life looked like success. He was a rising MMA star selected for The Ultimate Fighter on track for a career most people only dream about.

Then an injury changed everything.

A prescription became an addiction. Identity unraveled. The future he thought was certain disappeared. And like so many people navigating recovery, he faced the question that can feel both terrifying and liberating: *Who am I now?*

He didn't find the answer overnight.

He started small: volunteering, visiting children's hospitals, showing up where he could be useful. One day, meeting a young fan with a traumatic brain injury shifted his perspective entirely. Watching someone else fight a battle far greater than any he had faced forced him to reconsider what strength actually meant.

Being a fighter wasn't about dominance.

It was about service.

That realization began pulling him toward something bigger. Eventually, it led him somewhere most of us would never imagine going—deep into the Congo Basin rainforest. The conditions were unstable. The risks were real. There were warnings not to travel.

But purpose doesn't always feel safe.

Justin lived in a hut. He filtered every drop of water he drank. He ate what he could hunt. He witnessed hunger, disease, and systemic inequality that shattered his understanding of the world.

And eventually, the weight of it all became overwhelming.

Standing amid enormous need, he said he felt impossibly small, like what he was trying to do was the equivalent of trying to empty the ocean with an eyedropper.

The response he received reframed everything: Each drop represents a human heart. A soul. A life. Every drop matters.

That moment changed the metric. Impact wasn't about solving everything. It was about showing up for something.

That insight became the foundation for his organization, Fight for the Forgotten, which has a mission focused on clean water, sustainable infrastructure, and empowering communities long overlooked.

But perhaps the greatest transformation wasn't external. It was internal. Living among people who had almost nothing materially, Justin encountered something many of us spend our lives searching for.

He witnessed unbridled joy, even amidst scarcity.

Gratitude without conditions.

There in the Congo, Justin experienced the true meaning of community. And most importantly, he learned that gratitude isn't something you reach once life becomes perfect. It's something you practice so life becomes meaningful.

Justin's story struck me deeply because it illustrates a question many of us carry quietly: *What is my purpose?*

Most of us aren't standing in rainforests building water systems. We're managing careers, raising families, and navigating responsibilities. Purpose can feel like something reserved for extraordinary people doing extraordinary things.

But I've come to believe that purpose isn't about scale. It's about alignment.

When we're born, our purpose is simple: Stay alive. As we grow, the questions evolve:

Why am I here?

How can I serve?

What difference can I make?

I remember asking those questions intensely in my late teens and early twenties, back when I was filled with curiosity and whimsy. But adulthood has a way of pulling us back into practicality: earning money, chasing status, checking boxes. And somewhere along the way, purpose starts to feel optional.

It isn't.

Purpose isn't pressure. It's permission. Permission to align your life with something meaningful beyond yourself.

Purpose defines the "why."

Gratitude fuels the "how."

Without gratitude, purpose can feel overwhelming—like staring at an endless ocean.

But when gratitude is present, even small actions feel powerful because they're rooted in appreciation rather than comparison.

Justin didn't need to save the world. He needed to help one person. Then another. Then another.

And that's where transformation happens. Not in grand gestures. In consistent drops. Each act of service. Each moment of courage. Each choice to show up anyway.

Every drop matters.

When we're in alignment with our assignment—when we step into the role we're uniquely positioned to play—we stop measuring success by scale and start measuring it by impact.

Alignment with purpose doesn't mean your life becomes easier. It means your life becomes clearer.

You begin to see how gratitude and action reinforce one another: Gratitude gives you energy to serve, and service deepens your gratitude. And suddenly, the question shifts. Instead of asking, "What difference can I possibly make?" You begin asking, "Where can I pour my next drop?"

Because purpose isn't about emptying the ocean.

It's about honoring the drop in front of you—knowing that somewhere, for someone, it changes everything.

GRATITUDE PAUSE

Find Your Purpose (Without Overthinking It)

You don't have to know your life's mission before you begin. Purpose usually shows up after you start moving. Justin didn't set out to "find his life's mission." He simply started showing up for others—and purpose met him there. Don't wait for certainty. If you're unsure of your purpose, start with service, or try this:

- Notice what moves you. What breaks your heart or lights you up? Follow that thread—research it, volunteer, reach out, or take one small action that brings you closer to it.
- Start small. Purpose doesn't begin with changing the world—just help one person, or do one small, kind act.
- Test your energy. After serving, ask: *Did I feel more alive or more drained?* If you felt energized, explore it further. If you felt depleted, adjust how or where you're giving your time.
- Ask a better question. Don't ask a broad question like: *What is my purpose?* Instead, try something more specific like: *Where can I be useful today?* Small acts of usefulness create momentum—and over time, that momentum reveals patterns that point you toward your purpose.

Purpose isn't discovered all at once. It's built—one meaningful drop at a time.

V

Victim to Victor

"I knew we were about to have a long road ahead. But I also knew that from this moment on, I had to control the narrative and how we dealt with this together. I told my husband, 'I need you to swing by the house, pick up tennis shoes, and meet me at the park.' And that's what we did. We took the information outside. The power of nature, movement, and exercise cannot be understated. We walked and talked and came up with our game plan—and that helped me take my power back instead of crumbling."

—Samantha Harris, former co-host of *Dancing with the Stars*, Emmy Award winner, 2x breast cancer thriver, and best-selling author

*

Throughout this book, I've sought to give you next-level tools for enhancing your sense of gratitude and for employing that gratitude to improve your life in a variety of ways. We're not just trying to endure or survive a challenge but to grow through it in a way that feels meaningful.

So let's apply that perspective to the kinds of challenges that truly shake you—the ones that rattle your foundation and alter the way you see the world. Have you ever experienced something that felt like it redefined what "shook me to my core" truly feels like?

I have. And while it ultimately became one of my greatest catalysts for growth, it didn't begin that way. It began in fear.

It was an ordinary day in 2014 when I first sensed something was off.

I was sitting at my desk in my New York City office, halfway through a chopped salad, when my phone buzzed. A friend from my horse-show days texted: "Did you know Jack is saying some super weird stuff about you on Facebook?" (I've changed the person's name for privacy.)

Jack? I hadn't seen him in years. We had both come up in the equestrian world, orbiting similar circles but never particularly close. So the idea that he had anything to say about me—publicly—felt strange.

I logged on to look.

What I found was not mild gossip. It was a spiraling story filled with accusations so bizarre they might have been laughable if they weren't so deeply unsettling. He had constructed an elaborate narrative—one in which he believed I was somehow orchestrating conspiracies against him. At first, I felt confusion. Then disbelief. Then a creeping sense of vulnerability.

There is something uniquely destabilizing about being misrepresented publicly. It strips away your sense of control. And when the behavior escalated—when vague online rants turned into direct threats—that destabilization hardened into fear.

He posted a photo of a woman walking a Yorkie in Central Park—the same breed I owned—with the caption, "I'm gonna get you."

Suddenly, this was no longer absurd. It was personal.

I learned he was living just blocks from my apartment. I began altering my routines. I avoided walking alone. I felt my world shrinking—not physically at first but psychologically.

Fear changes you. It doesn't just scare you; it rearranges your posture.

You start scanning for danger. You replay worst-case scenarios. You begin to see yourself as someone things are happening to, rather than someone directing your own story.

In other words, you begin to feel powerless.

I wouldn't have used that word at the time. But that's what it was. My energy shifted from expansion to protection. I worried about how this reflected on my job. I felt embarrassed when colleagues became aware of it. I wondered if people would quietly distance themselves rather than be associated with someone who had become a target.

That sense of powerlessness isn't only about circumstance—it can start to feel like part of your identity.

For months, I lived inside that feeling.

What changed everything was becoming a mother.

There is something about protecting yourself that can feel optional. But protecting your child awakens a different level of resolve. My internal narrative shifted from "Why is this happening to me?" to "What do I need to do to protect my family?"

That subtle shift restored agency.

I began documenting everything meticulously. I consulted therapists, security professionals, and eventually private security connected to a high-profile family with whom I was friends. The laws around cyberstalking were still catching up to reality, and at times I felt dismissed. But I refused to stop looking for solutions.

Ironically, what finally drew law enforcement's attention was not the targeting of me alone. As his delusions expanded, Jack began naming public figures and high-profile individuals in his conspiracies. The aperture widened—and that finally prompted action.

Justice came, eventually. Jack was picked up by the police and began his journey through the mental health system. He was off the streets, getting the help he needed—and I was finally free of fear for the first time in what seemed like forever.

But the deeper transformation had already happened.

The experience taught me that while you may not choose your circumstances, you can choose your stance within them.

When we feel powerless, we often ask, "Why is this happening to me?" When we begin to reclaim agency, the question becomes, "Given that this is happening, who do I want to become?"

That lesson has followed me into other seasons of life—including those in which no external villain exists.

Because sometimes we slip into a powerless mindset even without a public crisis, without anyone actively harming us. We shrink in response to disappointment, insecurity, comparison, or fear of failure. In those moments, the shift from feeling like a victim to feeling like a victor becomes an internal decision rather than an external battle.

But there are also seasons when the crisis is unmistakably real—when life delivers something you did not ask for and cannot ignore.

And that is the kind of challenge Samantha Harris faced.

Samantha had already achieved tremendous success: serving as the weekend anchor of *Entertainment Tonight*, hosting eight seasons of *Dancing with the Stars*, appearing on Broadway, and landing on the covers of ten health and fitness magazines. Then one day, after a workout, she felt a lump.

The diagnosis led to a double mastectomy. Her daughters were three and six years old.

The news was overwhelming. Samantha had already lost her father to cancer, and other family members had battled it as well. She could not pretend nothing was wrong—but she also refused to let fear define the tone of her home.

She turned recovery into connection.

She began in-bed art projects with her older daughter. She transformed her physical limitations into games with her younger child. And when cancer returned ten years later, she faced it again—and beat it again.

Samantha moved from feeling powerless to feeling purposeful—not by denying the gravity of her diagnosis, but by choosing to use it. She became a certified health coach, an author, and a spokesperson for the American Cancer Society. Her experience expanded her mission.

What Samantha's story teaches us is that while we cannot always control what happens to us, we retain complete control over our attitude toward those events.

Mindset doesn't erase adversity, but it can elevate you beyond where you were before the adversity began.

This isn't about pretending your troubles don't exist. It's about extracting the lessons embedded within them and using those lessons to build something stronger.

When you reframe hardship through a victor's lens, two things happen: The struggle becomes more manageable, and the future becomes more expansive.

You begin to see that the very tools you develop in survival can become instruments of service.

I am not grateful for being stalked. I am not grateful for the fear.

But I am grateful for what that season revealed—the boundaries I didn't know I had, the resilience I hadn't yet tested, and the quiet strength that only surfaces when you are forced to stand.

If you are in a season that feels destabilizing—whether something is happening to you or something inside you feels fractured—know this: Being harmed or destabilized is an event. Staying in that powerless place long-term is something we can gently learn to shift. And choices can be revised.

The shift from victim to victor is rarely dramatic. It happens in small moments—when you decide to document instead of panic, to speak instead of shrink, to act instead of spiral. It happens when you realize that your circumstances may shape you, but they do not get to name you.

Victory is not about winning.

It is about reclaiming authorship.

And authors get to write the next chapter.

GRATITUDE PAUSE

The Energy Shift: *Why Me?* to *What Now?*

Sometimes when we feel powerless, we get stuck in the loop of Why me?—a question that keeps us circling fear, frustration, and negativity. But when we shift the question to What now? we take back a measure of agency. The shift doesn't have to be dramatic. It's often subtle. A small internal pivot that changes how you experience everything.

A shift from Why me? to What now?
From stuck to in motion.
From powerless to empowered.

Let's check the energy.

WHERE IN YOUR LIFE ARE YOU CURRENTLY:

- Venting instead of solving?
- Waiting instead of moving?
- Worrying instead of deciding?

POWERLESS ENERGY SOUNDS LIKE:

"Why is this happening to me?"

EMPOWERED ENERGY SOUNDS LIKE:

"Given that this is happening, what's my next move?"

To be clear, this isn't about denying pain or pretending something isn't hard. Some situations are unfair. Some seasons are heavy. This is about what you do with that reality—when you're ready.

Take one situation you've been circling.

Draw two columns and label the first column Powerless Response and the second Empowered Response.

In the first column, write the story you've been rehearsing—the frustration, the unfairness, the stuck-ness.

In the second column, write what an empowered version of you would do next. Not the grand heroic leap. Just the next available step.

You may not control what happens to you. But you can reclaim influence over what happens next. This is the heart of the shift: The situation may stay the same, but your relationship to it changes. When you choose an empowered response, even a tiny one, you interrupt the cycle of helplessness and remind yourself that you still have agency. That's where momentum begins.

Same situation.

Different experience.

Your move.

Witness Your Worth

"I always knew that I was dreaming way bigger than these shoes could fill at that moment. But I knew I was making these moves for something ultimately great. And I took so many courageous steps."

—Paula Blankenship,
American entrepreneur, author,
and CEO of Heirloom Traditions Paint

*

What are you worth?

Your answer to this question isn't nearly as important as how you approach answering it.

Some people hear that question and immediately reach for numbers—real estate, retirement accounts, investments, salary. Others calculate future potential: What they *will* be worth once the promotion comes through, the business scales, or the dream finally lands. Some measure worth relationally—as a parent, partner, friend, or community member. Others look inward and consider their contribution to society, their character, or the legacy they hope to leave.

None of those answers are wrong. All of them represent some expression of value.

But the deeper question is this: How do you value yourself when no spreadsheet is involved?

Gratitude invites us to acknowledge the blessings in our lives. Witnessing your worth asks you to recognize that you are one of those blessings. Not in a performative, affirmation-in-a-mirror way but in a grounded, embodied way.

What shifts because you show up? Who feels steadier, braver, or more hopeful because you are in the room?

Your worth isn't only financial. It's relational, emotional, energetic. It's the steadiness you bring during chaos, the courage you model without realizing it, the optimism that lifts a heavy moment. When you truly understand your worth, you move differently. You stop shrinking. You stop apologizing for taking up space. You stop confusing temporary struggle with permanent diminishment.

Witnessing your worth rarely happens by accident. More often, it is the result of courageous action, hard-earned lessons, and daring to believe you are meant for more—even before the evidence appears.

Paula Blankenship's journey to witnessing her worth was anything but traditional. She didn't graduate high school. She wasn't polishing résumés or climbing corporate ladders. Instead, she was skipping school, running her own secondhand store, and dreaming far beyond the limitations of her small town. Even then, Paula possessed something many people spend their whole lives trying to find: an unshakable internal knowing that she was meant for more.

Her creativity and relentless courage led her from designing small-scale, one-of-a-kind custom leather pieces to an almost unbelievable career break—styling country music icon Tanya Tucker for a major photo shoot using Walmart-bought leather and pheasant feathers. That bold, scrappy moment launched Paula into the world of celebrity styling, proving what she had quietly known all along: She was capable of doing extraordinary things, even without conventional credentials.

That pattern would define her life. Time and time again, Paula said yes first and figured it out later—from fashion, to home décor, to commercial interior design, to eventually founding Heirloom Traditions Paint. She was repeatedly told certain ideas were impossible, impractical, or unrealistic. But Paula never let someone else's limited vision determine her value. Instead, she trusted her instincts, embraced courageous action, and kept moving.

In her sixties, while many might have been tempted to slow down, Paula instead began showing up authentically on social media, and it paid off. Her straight-forward, unpolished style felt more like a comfortable conversation with a girlfriend and people loved it. Once again it seemed that almost by accident, Paula did something extraordinary by just being - and truly knowing - herself: She built a massive social following of over a million followers. By sharing an unvarnished version of herself, she taught her devoted audience how to transform their homes—and in the process, built a company valued at over $100 million.

Paula's story is not simply one of entrepreneurship. It is a masterclass in self-worth. She understood, long before external success confirmed it, that her value was never tied to a diploma, a title, or permission from others. Her worth came from her willingness to trust herself, take bold risks, and honor the bigger vision she carried within. Paula reminds us that witnessing your worth often begins long before the world sees it—and when you truly believe in your own value, you stop waiting for validation and start building the life you were always meant for.

I have witnessed that same reclamation of worth in the most personal way imaginable.

As I've mentioned before, my mother spent nearly two decades as co-host of *Good Morning America*, earning the nickname "America's mom." But her worth was never confined to reading headlines or interviewing presidents. It began with a quiet act of defiance that shifted cultural expectations.

In 1980, she learned she had landed the job at *Good Morning America*. Moments later, her doctor told her she was pregnant—with me. At that time, visibly pregnant women were often removed from on-camera roles. You couldn't even say "breastfeeding" on television, let alone normalize it.

So my mom walked into the executives' offices and told them she was pregnant and taking the job anyway. She also let them know that when the baby arrived, she intended to bring her to work. The executives stared at her, unsure how to respond—and then they said yes.

That yes changed everything.

Each morning, she would scoop me up at 4 a.m., breastfeed me in the back of a limo while reviewing her script, and then step onto live national television. America wasn't just watching a broadcaster. They were watching a working mother in real time, navigating ambition and family without apology.

Her impact extended beyond journalism. She became a visible example that women could pursue professional excellence and motherhood at the same time, in their own way. She interviewed four sitting presidents, reported from war zones and remote countries, jumped out of airplanes, landed on aircraft carriers, went behind the scenes with the WWE, and performed as a Las Vegas showgirl for a primetime special—all while raising a family in the public eye.

As I mentioned, decades later she'd find herself stricken with cancer. It became an opportunity for the ultimate reframe, turning this challenge into a springboard toward a new sense of purpose. She brought the cameras into the chemo room and shared her journey with millions watching, thus sharing an empowering message of hope as she bravely battled through.

In that moment, she reclaimed authorship.

She refused to let illness define her value. Instead, she expanded it. She turned vulnerability into leadership and fear into education. Watching her witness her own worth during that season was one of the most powerful lessons of my life.

Today she is cancer-free, joyfully known as "JoJo" to her grandchildren, still mentoring and speaking when she feels called. Retirement, for many, signals a decline in usefulness. For her, it simply marked a shift in arena. Her worth was never tied to a title, a camera, or a studio. It lives in her courage, her tenacity, her willingness to show up fully in whatever season she occupies.

That is what witnessing your worth looks like.

It is not bravado. It is not ego. It is not a résumé.

It is the quiet, grounded understanding that who you are—your resilience, your presence, your voice—carries value before you produce, achieve, or prove anything.

When you truly see that, something changes. You stop shrinking in rooms you're meant to influence. You stop confusing temporary hardship with permanent diminishment. You stop measuring your value only by outcomes and begin measuring it by impact.

Your worth is not a calculation. It is a recognition.

And once you witness it—really witness it—you will never again confuse your value with your circumstances.

GRATITUDE PAUSE

Reflect on Your True Worth

This exercise is meant to help you notice and name the many ways your worth already shows up in your life—not to prove that you have it. Before you begin, ground yourself in this truth: *I am worthy as I am, before I do anything for anyone.* The steps that follow aren't a measurement of your value; they're simply a way to explore how your presence, experiences, and qualities express that worth in the world.

STEP 1: NOTICE HOW YOUR PRESENCE IMPACTS OTHERS.

Not what you do for them, but how you affect them simply by being who you are.

Some possibilities:

- People feel calmer around you
- You bring humor to your workplace
- You check in on others and make them feel seen

STEP 2: IDENTIFY THE WAYS YOU NATURALLY EXPRESS CARE OR CONNECTION.

These are not obligations or measures of worth—just reflections of how you move through the world.

Some possibilities:

- Mentoring or coaching
- Giving someone a compliment
- Listening deeply
- Playing with your kids

STEP 3: LIST THE WAYS IN WHICH YOUR EXPERIENCES HAVE SHAPED YOU.

What are some of the big lessons you've learned? What have those things taught you about yourself? Which of those lessons are things that others could benefit from hearing?

STEP 4: RE-EVALUATE YOUR SENSE OF WORTH BASED ON THE FIRST THREE STEPS.

Now, step back and look at the full picture. This is your value—expressed through your actions, your presence, and your lived experience. This is your worth, not because you've earned it but because it's already there.

Ask yourself:

- *Where have I been discounting myself?*
- *Where have I been measuring my worth too narrowly?*
- *What would it feel like to fully acknowledge the impact I already have?*

Let this reflection remind you that you bring a lot to this world already by being in it.

X Marks the Spot

“I’ve found that people live in one of these categories: the Mundane, the Messy, the Madness, and the Magical. I teach people how to tap into the Magic on a daily basis.”

—Tim Storey, best-selling author and internationally acclaimed speaker

*

If there's one pattern I've seen after years of coaching people through transformation, it's this:

Most people don't fail because they lack potential.

They fail because they never launch.

They plan. They prepare. They research. They make lists. They wait for clarity, confidence, or perfect timing.

And while they're waiting, life keeps moving.

I learned this lesson early in my coaching career, back when I worked primarily in wellness and weight loss. One client—we'll call her Nicky—changed the way I understood what keeps people stuck.

Nicky wasn't lazy. She wasn't unmotivated. She knew exactly what she wanted: to feel strong, healthy, and confident. She just never actually did the work.

Instead, she became a master planner. She created elaborate food plans, detailed macro spreadsheets, and workout schedules that would impress any professional trainer. She would send them to me with pride, smiling as if the work were already done.

But she never followed through.

Some days she even faked screenshots of gym check-ins—which, ironically, took more time than simply going to the gym.

What Nicky struggled with wasn't strategy. It was belief.

At her core, she didn't believe she was capable of becoming the woman she wanted to be. And when someone carries that kind of internal narrative, no amount of planning will bridge the gap between intention and action.

Because launching isn't a logistics problem. It's an identity problem—one rooted in whether you see yourself as the kind of person who follows through, or someone who stays safely in preparation mode.

Over the years, I've seen this pattern across industries—from wellness clients to entrepreneurs, creatives, and executives. People spend enormous amounts of energy organizing their dreams instead of stepping into them. They say, "I'll start when I'm ready." "I'll launch when I know more." "I'll go for it once everything lines up."

But here's the truth most people don't want to hear:

The launch point isn't something you arrive at. It's something you decide. And that decision begins internally.

The clients who eventually succeed aren't necessarily the most talented or prepared. They are the ones who do the internal work first.

They become grateful—not just for what they already have but for the future version of themselves that they believe is possible.

That shift changes everything.

Instead of trying to force themselves into success through sheer discipline, they begin aligning with the identity of the person they're becoming.

That's what I call stepping into the magic. And by magic, I don't mean something mystical or unattainable. I mean alignment—the moment when belief, intention, and action begin working together.

Psychology refers to this as self-efficacy, the belief that you can influence outcomes through your actions. Neuroscience shows that when we visualize success and pair it with consistent behavior, we strengthen neural pathways that make execution easier. In other words, belief changes behavior—and behavior changes results.

Launching into something meaningful rarely requires perfect circumstances. It requires internal alignment first, followed by bold but intentional action.

People often ask me how I book high-profile guests for my podcast, expecting some elaborate strategy. My answer usually surprises them.

"I slide into their DMs and ask."

But the real work happens long before I press send. I retrain my thinking. I remind myself why my show matters and why the conversations I'm creating have value.

From that grounded place, I begin setting up the conditions that make a yes more likely.

When I invited Tim Storey onto the podcast, I was still early in my journey.

The voice of doubt showed up immediately: Why would someone at his level say yes? Instead of entertaining that narrative, I shifted into belief and action. I aligned my mindset with the outcome I wanted, and then I removed friction. I flew to California, drove to Orange County, and booked a studio myself so the experience would feel seamless for him.

Many people thought I was taking a risk that didn't make sense financially. But I understood something essential: Momentum creates magic. When you respect someone's time, show commitment, and move boldly, opportunities begin to respond.

I remember sitting in that studio on a warm California afternoon, adjusting my headphones while waiting for Tim to arrive. Through the glass hallway, I saw him walking toward me—or rather, dancing. His entire presence felt alive, joyful, and fully engaged with the moment.

It was immediately clear that he moved through life differently.

Raised in Compton, just outside Los Angeles, and shaped by early adversity, Tim could easily have become hardened by his circumstances. Instead, he chose gratitude. He speaks about life through four categories: the Mundane, where routine dulls possibility; the Messy, where challenges feel overwhelming; the Madness, where chaos threatens to derail us; and the Magical, where purpose, gratitude, and action align.

Most people, he says, spend their lives cycling through the first three.

The "Magical" isn't reserved for a chosen few. It becomes available when perspective shifts.

When you see obstacles as invitations rather than barriers. When gratitude grounds you enough to take bold action without needing guarantees.

Listening to Tim, I realized that the launch point isn't about eliminating fear or achieving perfect readiness. It's about choosing to move anyway. It's about believing that your dreams are worthy of action before the evidence arrives.

Magic isn't something that happens to you.

It's something you step into.

And once you do, the path forward becomes less about chasing opportunity and more about meeting it halfway—with belief, gratitude, and the courage to begin.

GRATITUDE REFLECTION

Launching into something meaningful rarely requires perfect circumstances. It requires internal alignment first, followed by bold but intentional action.

GRATITUDE PAUSE

Find Your Launch Point

Most people don't lack ambition—they lack a starting moment.

As mentioned earlier, Tim Storey describes four places we often live:

- **The Mundane**—safe, predictable, comfortable
- **The Messy**—growth, transition, uncertainty
- **The Madness**—overwhelm and overthinking
- **The Magical**—aligned action and momentum

ASK YOURSELF:

Where am I today?

Now, instead of trying to overhaul everything, use your answer to guide your next move:

- If you're in **The Mundane**, your launch point is disruption—do one thing that breaks routine.
- If you're in **The Messy**, your launch point is trust—keep going, even without clarity.

- If you're in **The Madness**, your launch point is simplification—choose one small step and ignore the noise.
- If you're in **The Magical**, your launch point is expansion—lean in and build momentum.

NOW SHIFT THE QUESTION:

Not *"What should I do?"* but *"Who am I becoming?"*

Choose one action your future self would take today—just one.

Send the message. Share the idea. Make the move.

ADD GRATITUDE BEFORE RESULTS ARRIVE:

"I'm grateful I'm becoming someone who starts."

Magic begins when movement does.

You don't need a five-year plan to find your launch point.

You need the courage to take one step before you can see the entire path.

Whether you're in the Mundane, the Messy, the Madness, or the Magical, the answer is the same: Keep moving.

Your Haters Are Your Greatest Teachers

"I lost a lot of time. Perhaps there was a blessing in that because it gave me time to reflect. And having the time where I really had to think a lot and reflect a lot, I was like, damn, I'm going to do something about this. I wanted to really take back my power."

–Nadia Ali, singer and songwriter

*

"Your eyebrows look like caterpillars."

"So sad you don't spend time with your kids."

"Getting a dog from a breeder tells me everything I need to know about you."

"Hope your kids like protein deficiency."

"Too thin. Too much. Too fake. Too privileged."

"Unfollowing."

When I first started sharing my life online, it felt like a giant, joyful group chat. My whole early persona was #fitspo, motivation, and the kind of bright optimism that helps people lace up their sneakers when they'd rather stay on the couch. It was workouts, wellness, family moments, and the occasional love story detail—like the fact that my husband, George (who is twenty years my senior . . . and is also my dream life partner who treats me like a queen!) proposed to me on a treadmill at Barry's Bootcamp.

Then one day, I posted something sweet about us . . . and someone wrote, "Ew, is that her grandfather?"

It stunned me—not because the internet is kind, but because my life felt so sincere. I had the instinct to clap back, to defend our relationship, to explain the nuance: The partnership, the respect, the shared values, the way we've built a life that actually works. But a creator I admired had told me something early on that changed everything:

Don't feed the trolls. Ever.

Because the hate isn't really a conversation. It's a hook. Haters don't want connection—they want contact. They want engagement. They want to poke your nervous system hard enough that you react, and then they get to feel powerful in the aftermath.

Over time, the hate comments diversified, as they always do when you're visible. Some people came for my appearance ("eat a hamburger!"), some came for my motherhood ("I could never sacrifice time with my kids for work, so sad"), some came for what I feed my children (mostly vegan), some came for where I got my dog, and some came for the age gap in my marriage as if love is only valid when it fits their spreadsheet.

I'd be lying if I said none of it ever stung. There were moments I wanted to retreat. And sure, in theory you can "log off." But if creating is part of your livelihood—part of your mission—stepping back isn't always an option. So I had to learn something else: how to turn hate into something useful.

This is where gratitude entered, not as a fluffy concept but as a nervous system tool.

When I'd get a nasty remark, I started pausing long enough to ask, "Where is this coming from?" And the answer was almost always one of three places.

Sometimes it was insecurity—the oldest trick in the book: Reduce someone else to feel bigger.

Sometimes it was a trigger—I represented a different choice or lifestyle, and my existence activated their discomfort.

And sometimes . . . it was grief dressed up as judgment. Someone saw a life that looked freer, happier, more expansive than their own, and instead of asking, “How do I create more of what I want?” they reached for the quickest painkiller available: criticism.

That awareness didn’t make me superior. It made me steady. Because when you understand the source, you stop taking the comment as a verdict . . . and start seeing it as information.

A comment about my kids? It reminds me to be grateful that I’m intentional about the kind of home I’m building. A comment about vegan food? It reminds me I’m proud of how we nourish our children—yes, even when my little Asher reaches for kale chips like they’re candy and whispers “gimme.” A comment about my husband? It reminds me to pause and actually appreciate the man who loves me well, supports my dreams, and treats our family like the center of his universe.

In other words: The hate doesn’t get to write my story.

It just accidentally highlights what I value.

And here’s the surprising part: Haters became teachers not because they were right—but because they were revealing. They showed me where I was still tender, where I needed stronger boundaries, where my confidence was unshakable, and where I wanted to deepen my own clarity.

Then I began teaching other people how to create content and build a brand online in a course I created called “Brand Ninja.” I assumed the hardest part would be technical: editing, pitching, negotiating, contracts, deliverables.

Nope.

The number one thing that holds aspiring creators back is the fear of being judged. Not by a brand. Not by a platform algorithm. Not even by failure.

By people.

A stranger in the comments. A coworker who finds your reel. A nosy Aunt Sally who says, "Oh . . . so you're trying to be an influencer now?"

And that's when I tell my students the truth with love: If Aunt Sally doesn't pay your mortgage, she doesn't get a vote.

You cannot build a visible life while waiting to be universally understood. You can't launch a dream while requiring unanimous approval. You can't be magnetic while trying to be uncriticizable. Judgment is the price of admission. And it's also proof you're in the arena.

This is the Brand Ninja reframe I teach: Instead of treating haters like danger, treat them like weather.

You don't argue with the forecast. You dress accordingly. You keep moving.

Because visibility is not the problem—it's the reward. If people can see you, it means you climbed high enough to be seen.

And that brings me to Nadia Ali.

Long before we were friends, Nadia was a voice that soundtracked my youth, the voice that poured out of speakers in packed nightclubs and made an entire generation feel something holy on a dance floor.

Years later, when I married George, there would be a full-circle moment. George works in the music industry, specifically in the dance music genre. Nadia was his client.

And thus, the artist whose dreamy voice I had listened to growing up became my real-life friend. Nadia became part of my world again through George and, eventually, as a guest on my podcast—this time, not as an icon at a distance but as a real woman. A mother. An artist. An entrepreneur. A creator who had to fight to keep her power.

In our conversation, she shared what it was like being a woman in a male-dominated industry—fighting for fair fees, pushing back on being undervalued, signing deals too young, and realizing she'd been treated like an afterthought in a project built on her voice. She told me something that hit me like a bell: No one is going to advocate for you better than yourself.

And then she offered the deeper lesson—the one every hater accidentally teaches if you're brave enough to learn it: The criticism, the obstacles, the unfairness . . . they can either shrink you or sharpen you. For Nadia, it lit a fire. It made her determined to prove she was the special sauce. It pushed her to build her own identity, invest in herself, and go all in—not because it was easy, but because it was hers.

That is what resilience looks like in real life: not the absence of hate but the refusal to let it steer the ship.

Your haters aren't proof you're doing something wrong.

They're proof you're doing something visible. Let them teach you where you still need boundaries. Let them reveal what you value. Let them remind you to advocate for yourself. And then keep building.

GRATITUDE PAUSE

The Hater-to-Teacher Reframe

Here's a quick practice for anyone who fears being judged.

STEP 1: WRITE DOWN ONE COMMENT (REAL OR IMAGINED) THAT WOULD MAKE YOU WANT TO SHRINK.

Examples:

- "Who do you think you are?"
- "Cringe."
- "You're a bad mom for working."

STEP 2: LABEL IT AS ONE OF THREE THINGS:

Projection (their insecurity)

Trigger (your life reflects a choice they didn't make)

Signal (a boundary or skill you can strengthen)

STEP 3: NOW TURN IT INTO A GRATITUDE STATEMENT THAT KEEPS YOU MOVING:

"I'm grateful I'm building a life I chose on purpose."

"I'm grateful I care enough to try."

"I'm grateful I can be seen—because I'm in the arena."

STEP 4: TAKE ONE "ARENA ACTION" WITHIN 24 HOURS.

Post. Pitch. Publish. Apply. Ask.

Small is fine. Forward is the goal.

Zesty Is Besty

"The fundamental truth is we're all uniquely and wonderfully created, down to a cellular level. I will never be you; you will never be me. You are already it. You already have everything inside of you, you just have to access it, identify it, amplify it. This seems so elementary, and it is, but yet we don't do that."

—Emily Ford, entrepreneur, branding expert, and world-renowned speaker

*

Throughout this book, we've talked about building gratitude as a foundation for living a bigger, more intentional life. Now I want to invite you to take it one step further.

I want you to lean into your M.C.E.

Main. Character. Energy.

But not the performative version social media sometimes celebrates—not the loud, spotlight-chasing, "pick me" energy that demands attention and collapses when it doesn't receive it. That version is exhausting. It mistakes volume for vitality, and that's not what we're after here.

I'm talking about something deeper: *magnetic main character energy.*

The kind that doesn't insist on being seen but instead becomes impossible to ignore. The kind that doesn't shout but radiates. The kind that leaves you feeling expansive instead of depleted.

For a long time, I misunderstood what zest and main character energy actually meant. I thought zest required being the loudest person in the room, saying yes to every invitation, pushing the dial to one hundred at all times.

If life was a party, I intended to be the confetti cannon!

But that wasn't zest; it was overcompensation. I was living in extremes—wildly up or painfully down—confusing intensity with aliveness.

What I now call "Spotlight Syndrome" looks shiny on the outside, but it's rooted in insecurity. It seeks attention without first building the internal worth to hold it. And because of that, it often attracts chaotic ecosystems—frenetic relationships, dramatic highs and lows, energy that feels combustible rather than constructive.

Recovery changed that for me. So did humility.

By the time I met the man I would eventually marry, I had settled into a different frequency. I was confident without being performative. Energized without being frantic. I wasn't chasing the center of the room anymore; I was simply standing in who I had become. And something fascinating happened in that shift: Instead of chasing attention, I began attracting it.

That's magnetic M.C.E.

When George and I began building our life together, we asked ourselves a deceptively simple question: *Who are we, really?* Not "Who do we want to impress?" *Who are we at our core?* We realized fitness had become our shared language. Discipline. Commitment. Growth. Showing up at 7 a.m. even when we didn't feel like it. Barry's Bootcamp wasn't just a workout; it was our church. It represented structure, shared challenge, and the kind of playful encouragement that strengthens both bodies and bonds.

Like many couples, as George and I fell in love, we'd have those late-night chats about what our marriage proposal might look like. Having both come from backgrounds in nightlife, at one point we considered an enormous, theatrical proposal at the EDM festival called Electric Daisy Carnival—fireworks, lasers, 200,000 people. Younger me would have loved the spectacle. But the more we talked about it, the more it felt misaligned. It was big, but it wasn't us.

True main character energy isn't about the biggest stage. It's about the truest one.

So instead, at 7:55 a.m. on a Tuesday, just after our final sprint on the treadmills, I heard a rather unusual thing said over the speakers of the sexy, sweaty "red room" where the Barry's Bootcamp classes take place.

"Everyone to your benches," the instructor began, "and George, down on one knee."

Before I could process what was happening, my mom and sisters burst through the studio doors. George was kneeling. I was sweaty, glowing, fully myself—no tiara, no nightclub, no costume. Just alignment.

I wasn't even wearing makeup—just the natural radiance of a woman in her full joy. Flushed from a hard workout, then recharged by the rush of love from the man who had just slipped a ring onto my finger and promised forever.

The studio staff burst in with pre-prepared protein shakes that proclaimed, "SHE SAID YES!!" down the side, which were passed out to the class. Photos were taken. A lifetime commitment was made.

It all felt so darn electric . . . in all the right ways.

That proposal ended up in the *New York Post*, Refinery29, and *Women's Health*. It started our public facing persona as a "fit couple," and because of it we launched a shared social media profile we originally called @NYCfitfam, which ultimately grew to a quarter of a million followers.

The reason for that growth? Authenticity. Our goal wasn't just to create an Instagram account but to build a community rooted in wellness and connection. We took the event-producing skills we had honed in nightlife—gathering people, curating energy, creating buzz—and redirected them toward something life-giving: workouts, mindfulness meetups, cooking classes, real-world community.

I didn't become someone new in that season of my life. I became more myself.

And that's what M.C.E. is all about—being so happy and grounded in who you are that your zest for life is contagious and invites others to join the party.

And that's exactly what Emily Ford captures so beautifully when she says: "The fundamental truth is we're all uniquely and wonderfully created, down to a cellular level. I will never be you; you will never be me. You are already it. You already have everything inside of you, you just have to access it, identify it, amplify it."

Access it. Identify it. Amplify it.

Not manufacture it. Not imitate it. Not perform it.

Main character energy, done right, is simply the practice of owning your narrative. It's making decisions from alignment rather than applause. It's setting boundaries that protect your energy. It's romanticizing your own life—not because it's perfect, but because it's yours.

Zest plays a critical role in this.

Zest isn't chaos. It isn't constant stimulation or relentless busyness. It's aliveness. It's approaching your life with curiosity rather than cynicism. It's believing that possibility lives not only in grand gestures but in ordinary Tuesdays.

When you live with zest, you don't abandon structure or responsibility; you infuse them with intention. You give yourself curiosity breaks. You try something new without needing it to become your identity. You take a different route home. You read outside your usual genre. You volunteer for something that stretches you. You wear the bold color. You host the dinner. You add texture to your own story.

Emily talks about frequency—how love, gratitude, and joy sit at the top, while resentment and shame sit at the bottom. Zest is an upward frequency. It is a deliberate choice to build your life in a direction that feels expansive. And when you cultivate that upward energy consistently, something subtle but powerful happens: You become congruent.

Congruence is magnetic.

When who you are on the inside matches how you move on the outside, you stop leaking energy. You stop scrambling for validation. You stop auditioning for roles in other people's stories and begin fully inhabiting your own.

That's what "zesty is besty" really means. Not that life should be louder or bigger or flashier, but that it should be fully claimed. A zesty life is one authored with intention. A main character life is one lived on purpose, not by default.

You already have everything inside of you. Your task is not to become someone else; it's to access what is already there, identify it clearly, and amplify it boldly.

When you do, you stop living as someone waiting to be chosen and start living as someone who has already chosen yourself.

That is magnetic. That is expansive. And that is the kind of main character energy that changes not only your life but the rooms you walk into.

Make it intentional. Make it aligned. And yes—make it zesty.

GRATITUDE PAUSE

The Daily Zest Test

Developing a zest for life is not a set-it-and-forget-it kind of thing. It's something you need to continue to cultivate. So, find some time every day to give yourself this quick Zest Test.

QUESTION 1: *HAS ANYTHING MADE ME WONDER TODAY?*

Have you encountered anything that tickled your curiosity? Did you spend any time thinking about it or exploring it? If not, can you go back and do it now?

QUESTION 2: *HOW AM I GOING TO SPICE THINGS UP TODAY?*

It doesn't need to be big or consequential—just intentional. Maybe you turn your morning coffee into a ritual instead of a routine, play your favorite song and dance while cooking dinner, or surprise someone with a spontaneous check-in.

QUESTION 3: *WHAT'S ONE THING IN MY LIFE THAT JUST TICKLES ME?*

What's something that happened today that gave you a little chuckle? What are you doing later that you're looking forward to doing because you always enjoy it?

GRATITUDE REMINDER

I want to live each day with a sense of joy and expectation.

Conclusion

If you've made it this far, I hope one thing is clear: You do not need a different life to experience more gratitude. You don't need a bigger bank account, a better job, a perfect relationship, a cleaner house, a healthier body, or a more impressive résumé. You don't need to wait for someday. What you need is a different lens.

That may sound simple. In a world that insists happiness lives just beyond the next accomplishment, purchase, or milestone, it can feel almost radical to suggest that transformation begins with perspective. But I've seen it happen—in my own life, in the lives of my podcast guests, and in the stories of people who have embraced these principles.

Gratitude does not change the facts of your life. It changes your relationship to them. The challenges may still be challenging. The uncertainty may still be uncertain. Responsibilities and setbacks may not disappear. But when you begin to approach life through a lens of gratitude, something shifts. You become more resilient. More present. More connected. More hopeful. You stop waiting for life to get better before you allow yourself to experience joy. You begin to notice that joy is already available.

And here's the beautiful part: Gratitude doesn't stop with you. Every time you choose patience over frustration, someone feels it. Every time you choose connection over isolation, someone benefits. Every time you extend compassion, encouragement, generosity, or hope, you create a ripple that reaches farther than you may ever know.

A grateful life is a contagious life.

Change happens through small moments, not grand gestures. One choice. One shift in perspective. One page at a time.

So as you close this book, my hope is that you remember to look—for the lesson, the opportunity, the goodness alongside the hard, the light that was never hiding from you.

One grateful moment at a time.

References

Berkman, Elliot T. "The Neuroscience of Goals and Behavior Change." *Consulting Psychology Journal: Practice and Research 70*, no. 1 (2018): 28–44. https://doi.org/10.1037/cpb0000094.

Calderone, Andrea, Desirée Latella, Federica Impellizzeri, Paolo de Pasquale, Fausto Famà, Angelo Quartarone, and Rocco Salvatore Calabrò. "Neurobiological Changes Induced by Mindfulness and Meditation: A Systematic Review." *Biomedicines* 12, no. 11 (November 15, 2024): 2613. https://doi.org/10.3390/biomedicines12112613.

Emmons, Robert A., and Michael E. McCullough. "Counting Blessings Versus Burdens: An Experimental Investigation of Gratitude and Subjective Well-Being in Daily Life." *Journal of Personality and Social Psychology* 82, no. 2 (2003): 377–89. https://psycnet.apa.org/doiLanding?doi=10.1037%2F0022-3514.84.2.377.

Karns, Christina M., William E. Moore III, and Ulrich Mayr. "The Cultivation of Pure Altruism via Gratitude: A Functional MRI Study of Change with Gratitude Practice." *Frontiers in Human Neuroscience* 11 (2017): Article 599. https://doi.org/10.3389/fnhum.2017.00599.

Lopez-Garrido, Gabriel (reviewed by Saul McLeod). "Bandura's Self-Efficacy Theory of Motivation in Psychology." *Simply Psychology.* Last modified 2023. https://www.simplypsychology.org/self-efficacy.html.

Ragan, Erica Pearse, "Thank You, Dear: Examining the Association Between Gratitude and Relationship Well-Being" (2012). Electronic Theses and Dissertations. 535. https://digitalcommons.du.edu/cgi/viewcontent.cgi?article=1534&context=etd.

Rusch, Heather L., Michael Rosario, Lisa M. Levison, Anlys Olivera, Whitney S. Livingston, Tianxia Wu, and Jessica M. Gill. "The Effect of Mindfulness Meditation on Sleep Quality: A Systematic Review and Meta-Analysis of Randomized Controlled Trials." *Annals of the New York Academy of Sciences* 1457, no. 1 (2018). https://doi.org/10.1111/nyas.13996.

Acknowledgments

This book was written in the space between life's highest highs and lowest lows—where gratitude became my anchor. I dedicate it to the people who stood by me, supported me, loved me, and helped me understand that truth. First and foremost, my mother, **Joan Lunden**. Walking through life arm in arm with her has been my greatest blessing, and this book exists because of her in more ways than I can count.

To my sisters, **Lindsay and Sarah**—there is nothing quite as special as the bond between sisters, and the belly laughs we share are on the top of my gratitude list each day.

To my husband, **George**—the love of my life and the greatest partner I could imagine. Thank you for holding my umbrella when it rains, both literally and figuratively.

To my two boys, **Mason and Asher**—you gave me a new understanding of love and purpose. Our daily gratitude lists, spoken out loud each morning, are among my proudest accomplishments.

To **Lou Aronica**, my co-author—because of you, this book made it across the finish line with grace and ease. This was a true labor of love, and your hundreds of hours of dedication carried it through so that the words in my heart could come alive on the page. Thank you.

To my spiritual recovery community, I am endlessly grateful. Without you, I would not have learned how to live in alignment with my purpose. The gifts I've received have become the lessons I now pass along—because they are, quite simply, the most powerful blueprint for living I have ever found.

Finally, thank *you*.

This book is my offering—shaped by all of you. It carries your fingerprints in every chapter. I hope it lifts you up in both the good times and the hard ones, and that you pass the message along to inspire someone else.

Because that's how this work lives on.

First published in 2026 by Rock Point,
an imprint of The Quarto Group,
135 West 36th Street, 13th Floor,
New York, NY 10018, USA
(212) 779-4972 www.Quarto.com

EEA Representation, WTS Tax d.o.o.,
Žanova ulica 3, 4000 Kranj, Slovenia.
www.wts-tax.si

10 9 8 7 6 5 4 3 2 1

ISBN: 978-1-57715-813-4

Digital edition published in 2026
eISBN: 978-1-57715-814-1

Library of Congress Control Number: 2026942099

Group Publisher: Rage Kindelsperger
Creative Director: Laura Drew
Managing Editor: Cara Donaldson
Senior Editor: Keyla Pizarro-Hernández
Art Director: Beth Middleworth
Interior Design: The Sly Studio

Printed in Huizhou City, Guangdong, China TT082026